spiritual

FROM VICTIM TO GODDESS

smackdown

Spiritual Smackdown: From Victim to Goddess

2025 fEMPOWER Press Trade Paperback Edition
Copyright © 2025 Jaclyn Shaw

Published in Canada, for Global Distribution by fEMPOWER Publications
www.fempower.pub | For more information email: media@fempower.pub

ISBN Trade Paperback: 978-1-998721-21-4
Hardback: 978-1-998721-33-7
Ebook: 978-1-998721-22-1
Audiobook: 978-1-998721-23-8

To order additional copies of this book: media@fempower.pub

WHEN GOD SPOKE, EVERYTHING CHANGED.

spiritual

FROM VICTIM TO GODDESS

smackdown

A MEMOIR

JACLYN SHAW

TO MY HUSBAND:

For giving me the story to write and for your unwavering support. Without the story, the wisdom doesn't exist. Without the experience, I would not be the woman I am today.

TO MY DAUGHTER:

As you birthed through me, I birthed through you. Thank you for giving me strength; thank you for guiding me in what I wasn't willing to choose on my own. Thank you for holding on. You are an angel in human form.

TO MY SON:

Seeing through your eyes changed how I see everything. From the moment you were born you've delivered divine wisdom straight from your soul into mine. You are an extraordinary blessing.

author's note

In bringing this book to the world, and sharing my story in this way, I've been filled with deep spiritual initiations. I've been called to go deeper in—in my truth, and deeper out—in my truth in ways that could have broken me. In ways that could have caused me to shut down, to hide.

It has required me to stand in my power, and stand in the conviction of my voice, when it would have been easier to stay small and quiet.

I have walked away from some very enticing publishing opportunities in order to keep the integrity of this story and my words. I was encouraged to leave parts of the story out—the parts that are "too shameful to be written in print for the world to read." I was encouraged to dilute my voice, to dull down certain parts, and to erase certain parts completely.

I refused to do so. Because I deeply believe speaking the truth about our lives is medicine. Our truth has the power to transform everything.

In ways seen and unseen.

This has been a journey of trusting in myself over anything and anyone else.

I understand many who read this book will have judgments about me, my husband, and my family. I understand there will be those who feel I'm "a disgrace to womanhood," something I was told when I first shared part of this experience on a podcast. A doormat. A poor role model.

Yes, I understand there will be people who agree this is a shameful experience that I should have kept to myself.

But who gets helped if I keep it to myself? Who gets served if I let fear and other people's judgments stop me?

No one—it definitely doesn't serve me, or you, or the collective if I allow the frequency of shame to live on by hiding my story and therefore diluting the experience for you as the reader.

I am who I am because of the experiences of my life.
Because of the wisdom delivered in the moments of my life.

I'm not meant to hide it.
Not any of it.

And neither are you.

And so no, I decided not to shut down any part of my voice because that would be a betrayal of my soul. A betrayal of who I am.

And truth is the only form of currency I'm interested in.

My desire is for every single person who reads these words to come home to themselves.

To return to the love within them.
To connect with their divinity.
Their truth.

To harness their personal power.
To trust in the sacred wisdom that lives within them.

Through my words, I pray you find a resonance in your soul.

My truth doesn't need to be your truth.
My belief codes don't need to match yours.

Multiple truths can coexist.

Through my words I want you to find the way to your truth, with unapologetic acceptance, unwavering conviction, and deep remembrance of who you are.

You didn't come here to be a perfect human being. You came here to have a human experience. You came here to grow and evolve at a soul level. You came here to remember you are both human and divine. You came here to experience being heaven in human form.

Remember that. Remember that you get to choose.

And there is always the choice to rise *from Victim to Goddess.*

xx Jaclyn

prologue

Throughout my Spiritual Smackdown, I had extremely vivid dreams, and I was sure they were foreshadowing events that were to come, especially the recurring tidal wave dream.

The beginning of the dream was so normal: I was walking along the beach with my best friend. I wasn't exactly sure where this beach was, but it felt like home. It was where the jungle and the ocean met, where the tide rolled in and out; it felt like my own little piece of heaven. The sun was shining brightly, the ocean was crashing in on us, and the sound of the waves brought me so much peace. It was just us walking on a totally secluded beach until we crossed through this small jungle trail. Then, everything changed. On the other side of the trail was a resort and busy beach filled with people. It seemed so out of place in what had just felt like a piece of heaven.

Nonetheless, we kept walking and eventually stopped to talk to some people we knew, then suddenly, with our backs to the ocean, we saw terror in their eyes. Everyone started running toward the hotel. It was complete chaos; the sound of the ocean waves was interrupted by screams of horror. I turned just in time to see this dark, murky, turbulent tidal wave about to consume us. Fear kicked in as I thought I was going to die, I can't survive this, it is about to knock me out. I started running for my life as well.

We made it to safety. In the hotel, we were protected behind a wall where the tidal wave couldn't come crashing down on us. The staff told us everything was going to be all right. No one died, the worst had come and gone, there wouldn't be a second tidal wave. This was meant to reassure us and to keep everyone calm, and it almost worked. But I had this feeling in my stomach that was telling me something different. That was telling me that this was just the beginning.

I wandered off on my own to an empty part of the hotel in a room resembling a glass box, with all four walls and the ceiling made of glass. I was standing alone in the center of the room when I saw the second tidal wave coming . . . for me. This time, though, it was different. This time, I was paralyzed by the beauty of the wave. It was not dark, murky, and scary like the first wave. This time, I saw the tidal wave for what it was. The wave was made up of the most stunning blue and turquoise waters. I watched it roll up one side of the glass wall, across the ceiling, then down the other. The colors were mesmerizing. The wave was strong, and powerful, but there was also something gentle, calming, and peaceful in the way it rolled across the glass ceiling. I felt safe there. I knew it couldn't hurt me. I knew I didn't need to run in fear. I was able to sit and witness the beauty inside the wave, and watching the wave open up was breathtaking.

WHEN THE ILLUSION OF VICTIMHOOD IS DISMANTLED,
PURE TRUTH IS WHAT REMAINS. THE STORY LOSES
ITS POWER AND LOSES ITS CONTROL BECAUSE YOU
SEE WHERE THE NARRATIVE CREATED LIMITATIONS
IN YOUR ENERGY FIELD AND YOU CHOOSE TO WALK
THE OTHER WAY. STEPPING AWAY FROM THE FALSE
NARRATIVE AND STEPPING TOWARD TRUTH.
YOUR TRUTH, THE TRUTH THAT LIVES WITHIN YOU.

intro

It's easy to choose the path of the victim.

It's not as easy to choose the path of the Goddess.

We've been taught not to.

We've been taught that God is working against us.

We've been taught to believe in a God that is punishing, in a God that is judgmental, in a God that condemns. We've been told we need to struggle and sacrifice.

But what if we've got it all wrong?

What if there are no villains?

What if there are no victims?

What if we've gotten God all wrong?

What if God wants what we want?

What if God sees truth and only truth?

What if God is on our side?

What if what we've been taught and what we've been told is the opposite of what is actually true?

Asking these questions is where my journey *from Victim to Goddess* began.

The journey that opened the portal to the divine truth within me . . .

The divine remembrance.

Divine love.

The knowing that I am, as you are, as we are, the all of everything.

All exists. Because I exist.

All exists. Because you exist.

All exists. Because we exist.

PART ONE

spiritual smackdown

chapter 1 | not looking for anything

I gave up on love before I knew what love was.

My heart wasn't open to love. My heart was reserved with barriers so strong that no one was able to penetrate it, and it wasn't for lack of trying. People tried. They definitely tried. But one after another, I shut it down. I shut them down.

There was a brief period of time in my early twenties when someone almost broke through the walls I had not so carefully built. He was so close. I could feel my heart opening; I could feel the tenderness; I could feel my desire to be held in love. And this person was so willing to love me, willing to see me for who I am, willing to hold space for me, willing to be patient with me, willing not to buy or feed into the bullsh*t stories I had been telling myself. But as he got closer and closer to seeing the parts of me that I had never shared with anyone else, I ran. I ran from him. I ran from love. And I ran more than once.

I ran because I wasn't willing to let my heart be held, because I didn't understand. My belief about love was that love was just a fairy tale, and life had shown me that fairy-tale endings don't exist. I was afraid of what love could do to me, and I was afraid of how much it could potentially hurt.

And so, I ran, trying to avoid pain at all costs.

I'm not sure where, how, or why I had established these beliefs about love. I grew up in a loving family that most—including me—would consider very normal. I don't remember ever not feeling loved, and yet here I was, an independent woman who was proud to say I didn't need love and I didn't need a man. I thought love would get in the way, prevent me from being who I truly was, and stop me from feeling free. So, I chalked love up to make-believe, people playing pretend, something that wasn't real. I wanted to live a life where the illusion of love didn't intervene.

I established the belief that love was a sign of weakness for those who weren't strong enough to be on their own, and therefore, love couldn't possibly fit into the storyline I was living. I didn't want to be seen as weak, vulnerable, or soft; I only wanted to be seen for the fierce, badass woman that I was.

What I can clearly see in hindsight is I was someone who deeply feared love, who deeply feared vulnerability, who deeply feared the possibility of experiencing pain.

And this is why I ran each time love presented itself. But I couldn't run forever.

God wouldn't let me. God knows how hard I tried. He knows I tied those running shoes tight, ready to run the full marathon, ready to outrun love.

But then I met Craig.

Craig who fit quite perfectly into the life I thought I was creating. Craig who was just supposed to be a good time, a summer fling. On our third date, I turned to him and said, "We are just having fun, right?"

I told him about the pact I made with myself to be single until I was thirty, which was still almost a year away. We were in agreement on what we were.

He knew I wanted to have kids someday, knew I didn't believe in monogamy, and never wanted to get married. I had seen it fail too many times. He wanted to get married but didn't know if he wanted kids.

So, that's how he perfectly fit into my life. In the long term, we literally wanted two very opposite things. But in the short term, we matched. I didn't want anything serious, and neither did he. We both felt free to be fully who we were, and it was extraordinary. We wined, we dined, and we talked at all hours of the day. On our second date, he whisked me away to New York City, not even trying to impress me; we were both simply in it for a good time. I truly don't think either of us realized we were falling in love. It was more "so if this is only going to last for a short period of time, let's make it the most epic experience it can be."

Fast-forward eight months (before my thirtieth birthday), and I found myself picking him up at the airport, wildly excited to see him, loving that he couldn't keep his eyes or his hands off me. I told him he could ask me to marry him whenever he wanted. I was ready to say yes.

Things moved quickly from there. We wanted it all: the house, the wedding, the marriage, the kids. He had caused my heart to fling wide open because he loved me for me, and he loved all of me. "He loved my wild," as my friends would put it. And I felt something with him I had never felt before.

His kindness.
His gentle soul.
His kiss.
His touch.
His love.
Him. It all felt safe.

The previous thought I had—that love was a fairy tale, that it wasn't real—well, now I was evidence of the opposite. I was living the very real fairy tale, and everyone around me was witness to it.

We did all the things in the way only we could do them. We bought the house, got married, got a puppy, closed my business and opened Craig's business. It may have looked like we were checking off boxes, but it was all done in a very much "us" fashion. Craig, who previously didn't know if he wanted kids, had a serious change of heart and wanted kids right away.

Eight months after our wedding, I got pregnant with our first child, and he fit right into our life from the moment he was born. We didn't change who we were or how we lived, we just did it with a baby in tow and with both of our hearts expanded. Because if there is one thing Kane did, it was that he definitely created more love between us. Every moment of every day felt like perfection.

Our friends who were also newly married and having babies at this time often asked me how we did it. How did we continue to live the way we did before becoming parents? How were champagne brunches still the norm? How were we traveling like we did? How did I get Craig to be so hands on with the baby? How did I have so much time for myself?

Fairy-tale Frequency, that's what it was.

And while there were a few disruptions in the fairy-tale life over the next two years, Craig and I were solid together. We were happy and we were in love. In love with each other, in love with our baby, in love with life.

My days were filled with all things Kane. We'd cruise the city, hopping from park to park to park. We'd hit the market, swim at the pool, hang out with friends, and spend hours upon hours cuddling up at home together. Craig would text me numerous times throughout the day, asking what we were up to, wanting more pictures, just dying to get home to us.

And those moments when he came home each day were the best. Seeing Craig and Kane together was an instant heart-stopper, and it had been that way since the moment Kane was born. One thing people had always been in agreement about with Craig Shaw was the size of his heart: it's massive, and it grew ten times the size when he held Kane for the first time.

Craig's chest was Kane's favorite place to be as a baby; Craig's shoulders were Kane's favorite place to be as a toddler. Everything was "Daddy, Daddy, Daddy." These two just fit together as if one didn't make sense without the other. And Craig couldn't get enough of it. It was Kane running to the door the moment he heard Craig coming home. It was the tiny pitter-patter of his bare feet running down the hallway in the middle of the night. We'd both hear him coming, and Craig would look at me with the biggest smile on his face and say, "Here he comes" as he moved over to make room for the little guy to snuggle right up between us. Those are the moments Craig cherished the most. The ordinary moments when it felt like nothing existed but the three of us.

Life was so f*cking good until the moment it wasn't. Until the moment it all changed.

chapter 2 | I knew before I knew

I knew before I knew, which sounds so weird to say in hindsight, because at the time, I truly didn't know that I knew. At the time, I felt blindsided. There were no warning signs, no red flags. But the moment it happened, I knew. It was a soul-level knowing that my human had yet to comprehend.

It was a period of time that lasted twenty-four hours. That's all it took. Twenty-four hours for everything to change.

I felt it first, that feeling that something was off, that feeling that something was changing. A feeling inside that didn't match the outside, because on the outside, it looked like one of our typical Sundays. A walk around the city pushing Kane in his stroller, a stop at our favorite brunch spot—minus the mimosas for me as I was eleven weeks pregnant—a play in the park where I snapped a few pictures of Kane adoring Craig and Craig adoring Kane.

But then there was the moment Craig leaned in to kiss me and I pulled away. My body was questioning things before I knew what was happening.

It felt like there was no buildup, but I'm sure there was. I thought we were happy because I think we actually were . . . or at least as happy as two people could be who were holding onto emotional trauma they had no idea how to process.

How do you process something when you're not willing to talk about it? How do you grieve when you're told that things happen for a reason, it's normal, it happens all the time, it's probably a good thing?

That's what I was told two years prior when the first baby died.

I got pregnant with our second baby when Kane was six weeks old, which was a dream come true. I'd always wanted a big family with my kids close in age to each other. Having two babies less than a year apart felt like part of the adventurous life we had curated for ourselves.

But sixteen weeks into that pregnancy, our second baby boy's heart stopped beating. The baby who appeared healthy and strong at an ultrasound just two weeks earlier was not ready to come after all.

It was a weird thing for me to feel ecstatically happy and devastatingly sad in the very same moment. And these feelings were amplified when I didn't naturally miscarry, my body unwilling to let go of this baby even though he was already gone. For two weeks I sat at home holding my almost six-month-old baby who was so full of love, so full of joy, so smiley and giggly, while also holding a baby inside me who was dead. The duality was disorienting, and like most things at the time, I kept it to myself.

Kane was the only one who saw my tears and my sadness. I didn't talk about it with Craig because he appeared to be fine, and I thought he agreed with what everyone else was saying: "Everything happens for a reason." It didn't feel like there was more to say. So, we just kept on living, the three of us, mostly in our little bubble of bliss.

And then one year later, almost to the day, we sat in the doctor's office again and were told our third baby wasn't going to make it either. This time, I was eighteen weeks pregnant, and there were decisions that needed to be made. Craig felt like there was only one choice, and while I agreed with him, I still felt like there was a choice. A choice between me and this baby.

This time, condolences shifted from "everything happens for a reason" and "the universe has a plan" to "at least you have a healthy child" and "at least you know you can get pregnant again."

Did that mean I was ungrateful for wanting another healthy child? I know this is not how anyone meant it, but it's how I received it, and it annoyed the f*ck out of me. It triggered things deeper within me, and there were elements most people didn't know. They didn't know I didn't actually miscarry. They didn't know that I chose my life over this baby's life. The doctors told me the baby had no chance of survival but that she wasn't dead either. They didn't know I had to go to an abortion clinic where I was treated brutally. They didn't know I felt like I had no choice. They didn't know that at the clinic they wouldn't let Craig be with me. They didn't know I had to be held down. They didn't know how heavily I had to be sedated. They didn't know I could hear myself screaming as my baby was ripped from my body.

They didn't know because I didn't tell them. Because I felt shame. Because there were moments I felt like I had no choice, moments when I felt like I made the right choice, and moments when I was sure I'd made the wrong choice in the very same breath. This is how I felt, and I kept it locked inside.

What Craig kept locked inside is his belief that karma was at play and over and over and over again he questioned what he did that resulted in two babies dying. He didn't see himself as the victim, he saw himself as the villain, wondering what he did wrong, feeling unworthy and like he was being punished.

There was no explanation for why we had lost the two babies. Both experiences and the conditions within the pregnancies were very rare. The doctor told us it was as if we had been struck by lightning twice and it wouldn't happen again. He said this with the hope of reassuring us, but here's the thing about being told you've been struck by lightning twice: it doesn't feel so rare. It doesn't feel like it's unlikely to happen again. It feels like the exact opposite. It feels like I am a magnet for strikes of lightning and so I'd better be prepared.

Obviously, this is absolutely not true, but the human mind can convince us of almost anything. It collects past data, and past evidence, then presents it to us as truth. And so often, we simply believe it. Without question we willingly believe the lies we tell ourselves. We take a fear or a worry and turn it into a fact.

Yes, we had two babies that died, but the fact was, we didn't need to prepare ourselves for this baby I was currently pregnant with to die too. But that's exactly what we did. We pretended we weren't, but fear was controlling a lot of the decisions Craig and I were making at that point.

So, when I say there was no buildup I could see, I mean on the surface. In the days prior to me finding out, there were no hints, there was no evidence that my life was about to shatter. There was nothing I saw that would lead to what happened next, but deep down there were patterns ready to be disrupted and healing that needed to take place. There was a lot that was ready to be excavated.

chapter 3 | finding out

It started with a fight between us. It wasn't even an epic blowout, but one of those annoying fights between couples that is a disguised struggle for power. The kind of fight where the only resolution would be one person being right and the other person being wrong. There was no meeting in the middle, no willingness to see each other's perspectives, no willingness to discuss. It was both of us standing firm in our positions, needing the other person to admit their fault in a battle for control. I was attempting to control Craig, which was not part of our natural rhythm together, and he did not like it.

So there we were after our Sunday morning stroll, after brunch, after the play in the park and the kiss that I pulled away from, stuck in this stalemate of an argument. Often in those situations, Craig would be the one who would end up giving in, but not this day. Not this Sunday that appeared typical and was anything but. This day he was going to hold strong, which led to us going separate ways for the afternoon.

I gave Kane a kiss goodbye, avoided Craig, and left. Stubbornness is definitely not one of my most attractive qualities, but yet somehow, I had been wearing it like a badge of honor since I was a child. I would not be the one to break.

I was fuming on the walk to my regular Sunday night yoga class, but the solo time was good for me. I typically went to hot yoga, but since I was pregnant, I had been going to a restorative class, choosing the Zen over the sweat. This is the night I found out people were right. You know, the people who say yoga is just as much for the mind as it is the body. Well, it worked. The time in class allowed me to clear my head, and on my walk home I realized the thing we were fighting about was actually ridiculous and I was ready to meet in peace. I sent Craig a simple text: "I'm sorry about earlier."

I figured this would allow us to slip right into our easy Sunday night vibes and pretend like nothing had happened that afternoon. But when I got home, it was clear that Craig was not feeling the Zen like I was. I asked if he wanted to talk about it, but he stayed silent, insisting that nothing was wrong. Saying he was under a lot of stress. I knew things had not been going well with his new business partnership, but it felt like something more than that.

I didn't pry, opting to trust that he would talk to me about it when he was ready. Trying to force Craig to speak had previously put up a steel barrier between us, and I'd learned to allow his retreat inward, knowing he'd come back to me when he was ready. As he was telling me nothing was wrong, he was putting on his shoes and saying he was going for a walk. He agreed to grab takeout on his way back, and I expected to see him in an hour or so.

One hour went by.
And then a second hour went by.

At this point, Kane was starting to get sleepy, and I was getting hungry, so we snuggled up on the couch. I turned on a movie for him and scrolled social media to kill time. One of the first things I saw was a post from a friend I hadn't seen or spoken to in years. It had a photo of her and her newborn baby. I hadn't even known she was pregnant. The last time we spoke, she and her husband were separated. Clearly, I was missing a few steps in her story. I sent her a message, congratulating her on becoming a mama and telling her to fill me in. She was online and got back to me right away, telling me about her move to another country, about how she and her husband got back together, and then how they ultimately separated again as she found out he was having an affair while she was pregnant.

Whoa! The first thought that entered my mind was: *Who would do that? What kind of man would do that to his pregnant wife?*

My second thought was: *Craig. Craig is doing that right now.*

My third thought: *That's insane. That's the craziest thought you've ever had. Craig would never, everyone knows that. We're talking Craig here. Craig, the gentlest, most loving, kind-hearted soul you will ever meet. There is not a person on this planet who has a bad thing to say about him.*

My fourth thought: *Where did this thought even come from? Look at your life; other women dream of this life.* In the past two weeks alone, we'd discussed future baby names, we had booked a cottage in the cutest little beach town for the summer, and we were in the midst of planning a trip to Disneyland the next month while it was still just the three of us. There was no way Craig was having an affair.

My mind said no way, but a stronger part of me told me to listen. You know this feeling. It was the type of feminine intuition that you can't ignore no matter how badly you want to.

I did know this feeling, and I knew it well. This inner knowing—my soul speaking before my mind had the chance to get in the way. I knew how powerful it was, and I knew I was never led astray when I tuned in, but I had no desire to tune into this. I had no desire to tune into this, and yet I couldn't turn away. I couldn't turn it off.

How many times had I previously said, "I knew it, but . . ." and "I was going to do that, but . . ." while ignoring my intuition because I didn't want to listen. Because I didn't want my intuition to be right. I could see all those times I didn't listen, all those times my intuition was there waving a red flag and I put blinders on, continuing down the path I was on, choosing the easy route. By shutting out the feelings, by not listening to the voice within, I was able to avoid the fears that came along with the truth. I was able to bow down and pretend I didn't know better. Then, when things blew up, which always happened when I tuned out, I could play the victim.

At that moment, I wanted to tune out so badly. I wanted to turn off my intuition. I wanted to go back ten minutes in time to the moment when I was cuddled on the couch and not scrolling on Facebook. I wanted to pretend those thoughts never entered my mind.

I looked at the door, willing Craig to walk through it. But he didn't.

I sent him a text to see where he was. I told him my belly was getting hungrier and hungrier and Kane was getting tired, but he was waiting for Craig to tuck him into bed.

He responded that he'd run into his friend Andrew, they were having beers, and I should go ahead and put Kane to bed.

I went into freak-out mode, which was not like me at all. Who did he think he was doing this to me? Leaving me at home at eleven weeks pregnant, with an almost two-year-old, while he was out drinking with a "buddy" I had never heard of?

I called him a dozen times before he finally picked up. I was ready to unleash on him. But he was beyond drunk, barely able to hold up his end of the conversation. He knew I was pissed, and he told me to calm down. He told me he couldn't handle all the pressure, and the last thing he needed me to do was use Kane to guilt him into coming home. I told him how confused I was. What pressure was he talking about? I also let him know how angry I was; it had only been two hours since he had left for a walk and to get food. How had he gotten so drunk?

He said, "I don't know." Then he followed it by saying, "I'm not coming home," and hung up the phone.

chapter 4 | no means yes

I didn't sleep that night. My thoughts were consumed with the very real possibility that Craig was having an affair, even though it seemed crazy. There was nothing before today that led me to believe in that possibility. No suspicious texting, no late nights at work, nothing out of the ordinary.

Craig came home the next morning just in time to jump in the shower and throw his work clothes on. He was in rough shape. I pretended to be sleeping while he was there. I needed time to sort out my thoughts before I confronted him.

It had been the longest night of my life, and I only had a short window of time to figure out the truth. My mom and sister were on their way to the city for the night, and I knew I'd pretend everything was normal as soon as they arrived. There was no way I would tell them what I was thinking. They would have thought I was just as crazy as I thought I was.

By midafternoon, I decided to just go for it. I sent Craig a message while he was at work, asking him what was going on. I told him I could feel that something was up, that something wasn't right. I reminded him about my spidey sense. He stayed strong in saying nothing was wrong, and that he needed me to lay off him and give him room to breathe.

I wanted to believe him so badly, so I suggested that we go talk to someone. Maybe I really was wrong. Maybe it was the pressure and stress he was under at work. Maybe it was his fears coming up about this baby not making it. Maybe he just wasn't willing to get attached, something I completely understood.

Maybe that was all I was picking up on, his fear.

Maybe he didn't want me to know how scared he was so he was shutting me out. I played back to the night just before we conceived our baby girl. He'd been out drinking, and when he came home, he broke down and wept about the babies we lost.

We didn't talk about it the next day. Maybe we needed to?

I let myself run with this possibility for a few moments, but then my inner voice shouted loud and clear, "Please don't betray me this time; please don't shut me out. You know I'm right."

F*ck. F*ck. F*ck.

I decided to be blunt. I sent him another text: "Are you having an affair?"

"No!" he replied emphatically, his voice strong.

"Are you sure? It feels like something is off."

"Absolutely not, Jak. I would never do that to you."

"Well, then, what is it? This is not like you."

"I've just been under a lot of pressure. We can talk about it tonight. I love you."

I wanted to believe him, but I didn't. At this point, there was no turning back. As crazy as it sounded, I knew I was right, and I needed proof. I slipped into detective mode, starting with Andrew, his new buddy I'd just heard of the night before and who Craig said worked at his gym. I checked the website to see when he taught his next class.

There was no Andrew on the schedule.

I gave Craig another chance to come clean right then. I called him and said, "I know there is no Andrew that works at the gym."

Without missing a beat, he said, "He's new; they must not have put him on the website yet."

"That seems weird, don't you think?"

"No, you're just being crazy. I'm not having an affair."

Maybe I was crazy, but I also knew I was right. As much as I just wanted to let it go right then and there, I couldn't. So, I called the gym and asked for Andrew.

"Andrew who?" the person on the other end asked.

Andrew who works there I wanted to scream, willing it to be true. But it was clear there was no Andrew. Instead of hanging up, I asked if I could book an appointment with the massage therapist. I was told she'd call me back. I left a fake name and fake phone number.

My intuition was guiding me. "She" definitely worked at the gym, I could feel it, which meant it was one of two people.

Either Karly, the trainer/gym owner's girlfriend, or Hannah, the trainer/massage therapist.

I was betting on Hannah, but time was running out on my day. My mom and sister were almost there, so one more time I went fishing for the truth. I told Craig I was finally booking an appointment with the massage therapist from his gym, the appointment he suggested I book two months prior.

He said, "That's great, babe."

Not what I was expecting. I had anticipated him trying to talk me out of it, but he didn't. So, again, I had to question myself. Was this all in my head?

I didn't want it to be true. But I also needed it to be true.

I had a deep desperation to prove my intuition right, although I was really hoping to prove it wrong. I needed to be right. I needed there to be a reason why I was feeling what I felt. I needed my feelings to be justified. I was on a mission and couldn't be stopped . . . only delayed.

When my mom and sister arrived, I pretended all was normal, all was good. I didn't let on that I was thinking Craig was having an affair. I didn't give them any reason to suspect anything out of the ordinary was taking place in our life. We had dinner together and all went to bed. But then I woke up the next morning more determined than ever to find out the truth.

It took less than an hour.

I figured out a way to access the contacts on Craig's phone from my computer, and from there it was simple. I found "Andrew's" number and called it. The voicemail that picked up said: "Hey, it's Hannah," and that was all the proof I needed.

My intuition the day before had been right. It was Hannah, the trainer/massage therapist.

At this point, I knew there was going to be no going back. There would be no denial I would believe. And I was not willing to sit with the information for one second longer because I was not willing to be lied to for one second longer. I drove to Craig's work and sent him a message, asking him to meet me out front.

My body was shaking. I was about to jump out of my own skin, but I was also oddly calm. I didn't give Craig a chance to lie this time. His contractors were all around, and I didn't want to make a scene. It hadn't even fully sunk in yet. I was still in disbelief, but I needed to know. I needed him to admit it, and I needed him to know I knew.

So, there on the side of the road at Craig's construction site, I shoved down the rage, looked him in the eye, and said, "Do you want to tell me about Hannah now?"

He could tell by my demeanor that I knew. It was clear I wasn't fishing like I had been the day before.

The moment I said her name, his jaw dropped, his eyes went to the ground, and he couldn't look at me. He had no words. That's all I needed to know it was true. "I don't know what to say," is all he said. And when he finally looked back up at me, I could see the pain in his eyes.

I only asked him two other questions.

"Does she know I'm pregnant?"

"Yes, she says it's none of her business."

"How could you throw your whole life away like this?"

"I didn't think I was. I didn't think about it. It just happened."

I turned to leave, and just before I walked away, I told him not to tell her I knew, and then because neither of us knew what else to say, I got in our car and drove away. I drove to a coffee shop just around the corner from her work. I knew I wouldn't actually go in and confront her, but I put myself in close proximity just in case I decided to attack. At this point, my focus was on her instead of Craig.

What kind of woman thinks it's not her business that the man she is having an affair with has a wife who is almost three months pregnant? I wanted to paint her as the villain, the evil seductress. Because if she could be the villain in the story, then my husband didn't have to be. There could be an escape clause. I could let him off the hook and put a Band-Aid solution on top of the whole thing so no one would ever have to find out. I thought we could forget that the past forty-eight hours had ever happened.

I needed to find out more about her so I could decide how to handle the situation. This led me to Instagram. It was the second time I had looked at her profile that day. I had checked her out on my way to confront Craig but only did a quick scroll. I wanted to go deeper. I opened up the app but didn't get far; her account had been switched to private. Obviously, this meant that she knew I knew. He had told her.

And this sent me into another downward spiral. I called Craig immediately. "You told her after I asked you not to."

He said it wasn't fair not to tell her. He needed to warn her.

Fair to her? What the actual f*ck. I didn't care about what was fair to her. Did he think about what was fair to me two nights earlier when I was sitting home alone with our two-year-old child, rubbing my own hungry pregnant belly that he forgot about feeding?

No, he didn't. I didn't want to hear him talk to me about fair.

I decided then and there to confront her. But Craig told me if I showed up at her work, that would be the end, we'd be done, there would be no chance of us fixing this. He told me to leave her out of it.

As if he thought he could call the shots. But I also knew he was right, just in a different way.

I wanted to blame her so badly.
I wanted this to be her fault.

I wanted to imagine that she was this seductive temptress and Craig was her prey. But that voice inside me had returned and whispered, "You know it's not about her."

And in that same moment, I had the knowing that it wasn't about me either. It wasn't even about our marriage. It was about Craig.

I also had this knowing that our story, mine and Craig's, wasn't over yet.

And although I had all of this knowing—knowing it wasn't her fault, knowing that it wasn't about me, knowing that our story wasn't over—my actions didn't show it. Because I also felt like I was a victim in this scenario. I had been wronged, which meant someone had to be held responsible. Someone had to pay.

My soul-knowing and human beliefs were in extreme conflict. And because I didn't trust in my soul-knowing, I responded from my human beliefs. I labeled her as the sinner and decided he needed to be punished.

I wanted to make them hurt as much as I hurt.

chapter 5 | fighting for us

By that point, I had figured out that I found out about the affair pretty much the moment it started. Like usual, my intuition was quick and on point. Seeing my friend's Facebook post and receiving that message from her after two years of not talking was not a coincidence.

And although I'd always been a woman who said I would never, I would never stay with someone who cheated, I would never forgive, that's what I set out to do. I told myself it had just started, so it could be fixed. It's not like they were in love. They couldn't be; it had only been two days. And before I met Craig, I didn't even believe in monogamy. Damn him for convincing me that monogamy existed.

I decided to walk over to her work but not to confront her. I knew she wasn't there. I had already checked her work schedule, and her not being there was the point. That way I didn't even have to say anything. I knew my mere presence in the building would get passed on quickly, and I was right. I stopped by her work, then started walking to our home, which was only two blocks away. Before I even made it home, I received a message from Craig. He knew, which meant she knew that I could show up at any moment. My warning shot was fired.

When I got home, Craig was standing in our living room. He said the babysitter had taken Kane to the park and he was ready to talk. He said that, but he had nothing to say. There were zero words coming out of his mouth. But I wanted answers.

"What were you thinking?"

"Obviously, I wasn't."

"How could you risk everything after all we have been through the past year and a half?"

"I didn't think I was. It just happened. I didn't think you'd find out."

Those words brought a sense of relief.
It just happened.
He wasn't in love with her.

I heard his words "I didn't think you'd find out" as "I didn't want you to find out; this was a mistake; it won't happen again; we can fix this."

But those aren't the words he said. He said, "I didn't think you'd find out; now we can't go back, it's ruined."

Then he told me he had to go. He said he couldn't stay because he couldn't look at Kane or me without feeling the guilt and shame he now carried. He said he didn't know what to do with those feelings. Those were the last words he said as he walked out the door with no plan to return.

And everything began to rapidly unravel from there.

I desperately began searching for the remote control. I wanted to hit the rewind button. Please tell me life comes with a remote control. I was at a complete loss.

Craig wasn't showing any remorse. It was like he didn't know what he did was wrong. The only explanation I'd received was "She said she wanted to be my mistress, that we could see each other a few times a month, and that you'd never have to find out. But now that you've found out, it changes everything."

There had been no: "I'm so sorry." No: "Let's fix this, babe."

The next time I heard from him was via text and all it said was "I'm going to take Kane to the park after work." But he didn't show up. It was up to me. I needed to do something to snap him out of this.

I needed to find a way to make him see her in a different light, so I went into detective mode and made it my job to dig up some sort of dirt on her so I could go to my husband and say, "Look at this. This is who she truly is. This is who you are sleeping with. This is who you are throwing your life and your family away for."

It took all of five seconds to find what I was looking for. Her sister had written a book detailing their single-girl life. It had *Sex and the City*-type vibes written all over it. The book, of course, was dedicated to Hannah and her wild-child ways. It was filled with page after page that described Hannah as a man-eater, detailing a previous affair she had with an engaged man.

This gave me all the ammunition I needed. This allowed me to feel justified in further vilifying her, and I made sure Craig knew it. I told him about the book the first chance I got, but it had absolutely no effect on him. I wanted this to sting. I wanted him to doubt his new relationship. I wanted him to see her the way I saw her. I wanted her to be the enemy.

I told him these things, but deep down I knew this wasn't the truth. I knew she was not some seductive temptress who was waiting in the shadows to prey on my husband. She was not chaining him to her bed. She was not the enemy, but it made it easier to tell myself that. To believe he got drunk one night, she pounced, and he made a mistake. Telling myself that story was easier than facing reality. It was easier than telling myself the truth: My husband chose to have an affair. He broke our vows. I was alone. I was pregnant. I was now a single mother of one, almost two kids.

His reaction to finding out about the book solidified it. He didn't care when I told him what I thought of her, what the world thought of her, what her own sister thought of her. I thought this evidence would wake him up. I thought he'd be turned off by knowing this about her. Then I realized this persona is what drew him to her. Her wild-child, not-caring-about-anything vibe was the attraction magnet. Overnight, he had decided this was what he wanted and who he wanted in his life.

I had no idea what to do next, so I booked a session with a psychic for some "channeled wisdom." It was with a woman who all of my soul sisters raved about, and I thought surely she would be able to offer me something that gave me peace. She did not. In fact, I ended that session even more enraged. It had been two days since my entire world fell apart, and when I went to her looking for guidance, she told me how much I am loved by God. She told me Jesus wanted to work through me. She told me that in my future, she saw me speaking on a stage, delivering messages about love, God, and universal truths. Excuse me, what?

I wanted answers about my husband and my marriage. I wanted to know if this other woman would ever exit our life. I actually didn't give a f*ck about God loving me and what Jesus wanted. I wanted what I wanted: my happy family back together. And I wanted this psychic, actually I wanted her spirit guide who leads the session, to tell me he saw it happening.

I wanted to f*cking know what happened next.

I was used to being in situations I could control, and I was used to getting my own way. In almost any argument, it was easy for me to come out on top, for me to convince the person on the other side that I was right, to make them see what I wanted them to see.

But not this time, not with my husband. I couldn't make him see that his family was worth fighting for, that we were worth fighting for. At the time, it wouldn't have even been a fight. I just wanted him to choose us.

I was lost and disoriented with all the thoughts swirling in my head. I was betrayed by my own feelings. Why didn't I want to tell him to f*ck off and be done with him like I'd always said I would if I ever found myself in this situation? All the times I had said, "I'd never . . ." So, why did I feel differently when it was actually happening?

In an effort to clear my head, I grabbed a pen and a piece of paper. I had never really written before and I wasn't sure where to start, but it felt like a good idea. I just wanted to get all the thoughts out of my head, hoping that once I did, they would all magically disappear. I didn't intend to write a letter when I first sat down, but this is what flowed:

JOURNAL ENTRY

Craig,

What happened that made you decide your whole life was worth giving up? You said you never wanted me to find out . . . you didn't want this to happen. So, what changed?

Where did the man I married go? In six years, I have never seen this side of you. Yes, I have seen the side that shuts down, puts up a wall, and keeps his feelings bottled in, but I have never seen this selfish person, this angry person, this mean person. You've never even said you're sorry. Are you sorry? Would you take it all back if you could? If you weren't happy, why didn't you just tell me?

I have so many unanswered questions . . . maybe you don't even know the answers. I don't care about what you did, it's your actions since that are what's hurting the most. It feels like you stopped loving me and started hating me in the same moment. It's like you've forgotten who I am, and who we are together. What happened? I'm completely lost.

You flipped a switch overnight. Why aren't you willing to fight for your family, to talk to someone, to get help? You not only walked out on me, but you walked out on Kane too. He misses you, he needs you. I can't even imagine what's going through his head and how confused he is. It's actually killing me.

Don't you remember the mornings, the middle of the nights he'd crawl into bed with us? When he'd come downstairs on the weekends and be so excited you were home in the mornings? His reaction when you'd come home from work? How are you okay with being two blocks away and not dying to see him every day? Don't you miss his giggles and smiles, playing with him, his goodnight kisses?

You've always said he is your whole world, that you'd do anything for him. Did those feelings go away too?

I want Kane to have his amazing dad back. I want our daughter to experience that kind of love and bond with you, but I feel like you don't even want her . . . I'm so worried about her.

You seem to be following in your father's footsteps. Don't you want to break that cycle? You try to pretend it doesn't bother you, but I know how much pain him leaving caused you. Don't you want to be different?

You are just living in the now. What about down the road? Even now, how are you so suddenly okay with being a part-time dad? What changed? Why are you so eager to close this chapter of your life?

Do you remember how badly you wanted to be a parent after we got married? More so than me. You are a great dad . . . you've loved being a dad. Being a dad changed your heart. Now you've closed it again.

I worry for our kids and myself, but I also worry for you. I worry you are going to wake up one day and be a very sad, lonely, depressed man. I don't want that for you.

You are at a crossroads right now. You can face this, talk to someone, and finally heal, which will allow you to be the man and father who I truly believe you want to be.

Have you already gone too far down the other path? I don't think so, but I know you do. I see so much darkness down that road for you. I can't pull you out; you have to do that. But I can be here to support you and love you if you let me. Open your heart back up to me, let me in, talk to me.

I said for better or worse. I can love you through this, and I truly believe we will come out stronger on the other side with a deeper, more meaningful love and life.

Let this be a rebirth for you. For us! Don't shut your heart off. Yesterday, you told me you loved me. Did you mean it?

Fight For Us!

I didn't send this letter. I wrote it more for me, than him. In that moment, it helped to express these words and to acknowledge the unexplainable feeling I had that our story together wasn't over.

Moments later, this was verified. As I wandered aimlessly around the city, pushing our child in his stroller, thinking how my life had changed, I experienced a voice taking over my body. A voice that said I was going to be okay, and for a fraction of a second, I felt peace. I felt a knowing that I would be okay, that our kids would be okay, that we would be okay.

I pulled out my phone and sent Craig a message: "I don't know how, but I know we're going to be okay."

He responded right away: "I know you and the kids will be okay." No we, no us. Me, separate from him.

This is the moment everything fully hit me.

Villainizing her wasn't working and rationalizing with him wasn't working. So, feeling desperate, feeling like I needed to do something drastic to shake him out of whatever he was thinking, I decided to deprive him of us. Because I couldn't imagine that he could imagine a life without his child being part of his every day.

chapter 6 | running shoes

I put on my running shoes, and I ran. It's the thing I'm good at. When things get too uncomfortable, I run away. I've been doing it forever. Not literally, of course. I packed a bag for Kane and me and booked a flight to Florida that was scheduled to leave in three hours. That was my version of running, fleeing to another country. I told Craig that Kane and I were going away for a few days so he could figure his life out and end his affair so we could go back to normal.

I didn't tell anyone what was going on. I couldn't. Like everyone else, my family has always loved Craig. It would kill them to know, and I didn't want them to look at him differently once this all blew over. I didn't feel like I could tell my friends either. Everyone thought Craig and I had the perfect marriage.

I told myself I didn't know how to tell anyone, I didn't know what to say, but mostly, I was afraid of the judgment I would face. What would people think about me if my perfect husband could just run off with another woman while I was three months pregnant? I definitely thought people would assume I must be a real b*tch.

Shame flooded all over me. I was so embarrassed and so hurt. I felt like I had no one to turn to, even though that wasn't true. It was my ego getting in the way.

I got on that plane, feeling exhausted, alone, and scared. I hung on to Kane as tightly as I could, vowing to be strong for him. He was not even two yet, and we had already been through so much together. He helped me hold it together during both my miscarriages. He would help me get through this too.

Florida was a disaster. I was consumed with thoughts of Craig all day and all night. How did it start? What was he thinking? What was he doing in that moment? Was he with her? How had I been so blindsided? I was continuing to deal with this on my own and I was drowning, but I pretended nothing was wrong. When our friends and family asked about the spur-of-the-moment trip, I simply said that winter was getting depressing, and we needed the beach, the ocean, and the sunshine.

And I cued up all the Instagram-worthy pictures of Kane and me on the beach having the time of our lives on our spontaneous trip to Florida. #beachbumlife No one noticed I'd lost twelve pounds, dropping from 120 to 108 in less than a week. I couldn't eat or sleep, which led to more anxiety. I knew that my choices weren't great for the baby growing inside of me. I wondered how she was going to survive while I was such a disaster on both a physical and emotional level. And I compounded the anxiety when I worried about how my stress and negative energy was going to affect her.

It's just a few days I told myself, thinking that once we'd return home, everything would go back to normal. I hung on to the fact that no one knew, the belief Craig and I could fix this and pretend it never happened.

Each day from sunrise to sunset, Kane and I hung out on the beach. He was so happy, running in the sand, dipping in and out of the ocean. I watched him while experiencing tidal waves of emotions. I'd go from happy to sad to shocked to angry to total disbelief within a matter of seconds. I shed a million tears on that beach, wondering where Craig and I took such a wrong turn. I felt defeated.

From the beach, I had another session with the psychic, the same one from before. As soon as we got started, it was clear why the session was being delivered in two parts. The fact that she talked about God and Jesus, well, I needed to work that out within myself because at the time, God was not a word I would even use. I also needed time in between the sessions to work up the courage to ask the question I really wanted to ask. The question I was so scared to ask.

I resisted.
And Jesus waited.

I resisted some more.
And Jesus waited some more.

It got to the point that it was wildly uncomfortable. The woman said this had never happened before and she wasn't clear on why Jesus was waiting, on why nothing was coming through.

I whispered, "I know why. He's waiting for me to ask the question I don't want to ask."

"He's willing to give you your answer but only if you're willing to ask the question."

Through streams of tears I asked, "Is this woman going to be in our lives forever?"

Jesus responded with a swift no. And that was it—a small glimmer of hope.

This was followed by another glimmer of hope when I received a text from Craig that said: "I miss you two." My heart instantly swelled, and I responded: "Don't you mean us three?" He told me he kept forgetting about the little munchkin growing inside me. He also confirmed what I had suspected: that he was afraid to get attached to her.

As we were texting, he started a video call so he could see Kane on the beach. The two of them love each other so much. Moments after we hung up, Craig sent another text: "I love you. We are going to figure this out."

Finally, I could breathe, and I ate for the first time in days. My heart had been telling me it would be okay, but my mind kept spiraling to all the worst-case scenarios. That night, I crawled into bed knowing I'd finally be able to fall asleep, and I did . . . until my phone rang at 3:14 a.m. I said hello, but no one responded. They didn't hang up either. All I could hear was two drunk girls' muffled voices and their high heels clicking on the sidewalk.

This sent my whole body into a panic. I got those butterflies you feel deep in your stomach, and I thought I was going to be sick. I knew something bad was happening and tried to call Craig. He didn't answer, so I pulled out my computer and checked his email. I had become that person who checks their partner's emails, phone bills, and credit cards statements without him knowing I had access to any of it.

And there it was. At 3 a.m. on a Saturday night, less than a week since the affair had started, and Craig had just booked himself a trip to an adults-only resort in Mexico. It was leaving in three weeks, the day after Kane's second birthday. Less than twelve hours after he told me he loved me. I knew I'd lost him.

I knew he truly wasn't coming home.

The next day, we returned to Toronto in the middle of the night, and Craig was not at the airport waiting for us. He was not at home either. Feeling defeated, I sent him a message that said: "So, you're leaving me for another woman. You're walking away from your pregnant wife, your two-year-old, and your unborn child?"

He only needed one word to respond: "Yes."

chapter 7 | choosing shame

I couldn't keep going like this. I couldn't keep fighting. I couldn't keep doing this on my own, and yet I had no one to turn to because no one knew. I still hadn't told anyone, and I didn't plan to. What would I say? What would they think?

It's interesting how we do this to ourselves, isn't it? How we experience shame and how we choose to isolate because of it.

I chose shame.

I chose hiding.

I chose suffering in silence, not allowing myself to be supported by people who love me because I was worried about what they would think. I was worried about how other people would look at me. I made up all sorts of stories about what they would say. "They" who I don't even know, because I was making it all up. I was making them up.

chapter 8 | trying to hold on

It felt like my inside and my outside weren't matching up. Inside, I continued to feel that this wasn't the end of us, that our story wasn't over, that I was going to be okay. But my exterior world was telling me the opposite, Craig was telling me the opposite, and he was living as if we were done.

When we got back from Florida, Craig and I agreed to meet and discuss our future and where to go from here. I wasn't sure what to expect from him, but as we slid into a booth at one of our favorite restaurants, I felt him . . . the him I knew, the him who was soft, caring, loving. He didn't show up in the rigid, stern demeanor I had recently gotten used to, with the stone-cold eyes. It felt like it was him and me, and we were both open to talking. *Thank God*, I thought—but not actually meaning God. God is not a word I would ever use like that.

We agreed to not lead with our fiery emotions but just pure truth. I asked him to give us a chance, to give our family a chance, our baby girl a chance, and to not throw it all away for someone he barely even knew.

He showed up to talk, to finally have a real conversation, but he also made it vividly clear that there was only one way for us to move forward, and that was not together. He had decided to own his choice. He declared it wasn't a mistake, this was what he wanted, and she was who he wanted in his life.

I wasn't going to let that be the end of the conversation. "Why didn't you tell me you were unhappy?"

"I didn't even know I was unhappy, but I must have been or why else would I do this?"

"You said that you didn't intend for me to find out. Don't you think that means something? You didn't want me to find out, which means you didn't want our marriage to end. Why are you so sure about us being over now?"

"Because you did find out and now there is no turning back."

He'd agreed to meet with me to tell he would be there for his kids but wanted nothing to do with me. He didn't actually say this second part, but this is how it hit me.

What he actually said was "I love you and of course I always will. You are the mother of my children." Blah, blah, blah is all I heard because at the end of him telling me he would always love me and be there for me and the kids, he also said, "But I want to be with her more, and I can't imagine my life without her."

Essentially, what he was saying was he wanted a quick and tidy divorce, he wanted me to accept it, and he wanted to move on. I didn't let go so easily, though. Not at all. I begged and I pleaded. Their affair had just started. He couldn't love her already, he loved me—he had just said it.

Desperation entered at this point. I was desperate to hang on to my marriage, and not even because of how great it was, which it truly was, but because I was afraid. I was afraid of the impact this would have on Kane and my unborn daughter. I was afraid of failing, and at that point, I lived by a strict standard of success. Failure was literally not an option in my world. And mostly, I continued to be afraid of the judgment from others.

Again, I told him we could get past this, that in five years we wouldn't even remember her name. I offered for him to continue seeing her but to stay married to me, reminding him that when we first met, I didn't even believe in monogamy. But he said it wouldn't be fair to her.

I was so tired of hearing him talk about what was fair and not fair to her, without thinking about what was fair to me, his pregnant wife, the one he took vows with. I was so annoyed that he didn't think about what was fair to his son, the one he absolutely adored and who absolutely adored him. And then, what about how not fair it was to our daughter, the one we hadn't even met yet? I questioned how we'd ever explain this to her. How it would affect her, knowing she was abandoned before she was even born.

We didn't ask for this. How could he not see this? How was he not seeing what I wanted him to see? How was he not choosing what I wanted him to choose?

He wasn't just leaving me, it felt like he was leaving all of us.

He assured me that wouldn't happen. He said he'd be there for us, and we would raise our kids together.

I heard his words; I understood perfectly well what he was saying. He wanted us to be at peace, he wanted to be there for our kids, but he wanted us to be over. He was fully moving in with her, his girlfriend of two weeks. You'd think I would have given in here, but I didn't. I heard his words, and I still resolved to fight.

To fight for him, to fight for us, to fight for our family.

I started describing Craig as Jekyll and Hyde. It seemed like every time he showed up to spend time with Kane, he was angry. He didn't even look like himself, and I wasn't the only one who noticed it. Our friends had noticed it too. I swear his eyes changed color; they were darker, almost black. His body language was different, and the words that came out of his mouth didn't even sound like him. There was a new tone in his voice. He acted differently; he was cold. I'd never met this version of Craig before, and it was a version of him I didn't want to know. I wanted the Craig I knew to come back.

This is when I began to see a pattern. I started to notice a shift in him, one of the moments when the glimmer of hope shined through. After he would spend a few hours with Kane, his whole demeanor would change: he softened, his eyes got lighter, he'd smile again, and he'd be gentle with me, the me who he was perpetually angry toward. I'd feel his tenderness, and it felt like a miracle.

I took advantage of one of these moments and instigated our first real conversation in what seemed like forever. I started by asking him a simple question: "Are you happy?"

I want to say his response surprised me, but it didn't. I knew he had been wearing a mask.

"How could I be?"

"Do you ever regret your decision? Do you ever think you made a mistake?"

"All the time. Every time I see you guys, I remember how much I love you."

This brought up feelings of relief and deep sadness, along with my desire to know more about what he was feeling. "What happens after that? What happens when you leave?"

"I just shut down. I turn it off, like a switch."

He explained it was easy for him to do because he had his new life to turn to, a new life that distracted him, a new life that was busy, filled with people and parties. And then he added this part: "I don't feel the guilt there, the guilt I feel every time I look at you guys."

My tears started to flow, aching over the pain in his voice and feeling the sadness that existed between us. Then I asked him if he wanted to run away forever. It was easy to see what he was doing. We both knew it: he was chasing pleasure to avoid his pain.

I asked him if he wanted to feel like that forever. And I told him the way I saw it, he had a choice. He could face this now, or he could do what was natural to him, what had been modeled to him: repeat the patterns of his family and do what his father did—leave.

He agreed; he knew he was taking the easy route. He said he didn't want to just run away. We decided we would go talk to someone, together. This felt like a prayer being answered. I booked us the next available appointment that was two weeks away.

But just as quickly as this opening came, it closed again. I found a note from her to him that said, "I love you sooooooooo much, muffin face," and I turned into a petty b*tch.

It had only been three weeks since their affair started, so how could she love him sooooooooo much already? She barely even knew him.

chapter 9 | her

To you; you know exactly who you are.

Did you realize you were destroying a whole family? If you knew my son and knew the relationship he and Craig have, I don't know how you'd live with yourself.

I know you don't know me, and you don't owe me anything, but what went through your mind knowing I was pregnant? Does it not bother you now, knowing I am carrying Craig's daughter?

I get that you slept with him . . . maybe there was a thrill for you to engage with a married man, but you then asked him to leave his pregnant wife and CHILD! You were so eager to accept him with open arms, and now you love him? Really???? If you truly loved him, wouldn't you want him to be with his family, with his child? Wouldn't you encourage that?

I also wonder whether this is really what you signed up for? You went from having a short affair—let's be real, it was three days—to letting my husband move in with you. Did you sign up for all that comes with Craig? Do you want to meet my kids? Do you want to play stepmom? Do you really want to deal with me for the next twenty years of your life?

Have you thought this through? Or are you just hoping Craig walks away from his kids too? Do you want to start a life with a man who would do that?

I don't think you have any idea the joy you are robbing Craig of. He shines as a father. I feel like this is fun for you now. I know how charming Craig is, how great he is, how these trips and dates feel so amazing, I am literally watching him date you the way he dated me. He is taking you on the same dates, literally to the same spots. You are walking in my energetic footprint. It's fun, isn't it? But reality will set in at some point. He is going to have to deal with his wife and family eventually. It's been three weeks. Is it really worth it to you? How can you "LOVE" him soooooooooo much already?

Do you really not care that you have separated him from his son and unborn daughter? Do you not have any sense of family? I guess I can answer that one myself. I've read the book and I know the answer to this is no. Your daddy left you and you've been desperate for a man's attention ever since. You will take whatever you can get.

Again, I didn't actually send the letter. But I hoped she felt it. I hoped my words got translated to her through the ethers. I was ready for her to wake up to her new f*cking reality, and to recognize the glass slipper didn't actually fit.

chapter 10 | manipulation tactics

It had only been three weeks, but it felt like three years. I was ready to put an end to it. An end to him and her. I was ready to go lower, to do whatever it took. Obviously, he didn't care what I told him about her, but maybe she'd care what I told her about him.

Before their adults-only trip, I started to have a feeling that Craig lied to me about her knowing I was pregnant, so I asked him if I could meet her. I used Kane as the reason why, saying I wanted to meet her before he introduced her to our son. He responded with an immediate no. No, I couldn't meet her; he didn't think it was a good idea. As I suspected, as much as Craig was trying to hide her from me, he was also trying to hide me from her.

So, with petty bitch−mode activated, I put a plan in place to make sure she became fully aware of just how pregnant I was. It was pretty easy to do. Her sister and I shared a mutual friend. My friend told the sister, the sister told Hannah, and from there, I sat back and watched the fireworks explode. No one could trace the game of telephone back to me, and even if they could, Craig would have nothing to say. To get mad at me would mean he'd have to admit he lied about her knowing in the first place.

I let the bomb drop and then put my running shoes back on, thinking this time, depriving him of us would have a different effect. It was the same manipulation tactic, but with this new development in the story, I thought it would create a different result.

So, the day before Kane's second birthday, he and I flew to the west coast to visit my best friend. Craig was not overly happy about this because he'd delayed his trip to Mexico by two days so he'd be home for Kane's birthday. I decided that this wasn't how it was going to work, though. He FaceTimed on Kane's birthday, but after that, I left every message he sent unread. I wasn't going to let him have his cake and eat it too.

I decided when he was with her, he didn't get us. I thought maybe if he didn't hear from us for two weeks, maybe if he experienced what it was like to watch our life in pictures on social media, he'd wake up and realize what he was giving up. I wanted him to feel this pain. I wanted him to feel regret. I wanted him to realize that she wasn't worth him losing us.

Stoning him out didn't work, though, and it, paired with the stunt to get the memo to her that I was pregnant, created a bigger divide between us. Our communication broke down completely. A full barrier went up between us, and Craig bailed on our first appointment to see the mediator.

We were in a battle for power, both trying to control and manipulate the situation.

Feeling helpless, and not sure where to turn, I went to see the family mediator on my own. I told her about everything going on, and she said while it was not going to be the most productive way to sort some things out between Craig and me, it also may not be a bad thing for us to start off seeing her individually. When she asked me what I wanted from Craig, I told her truthfully, at that point, I wanted there to be peace.

I was so exhausted by Craig's Jekyll and Hyde behavior, his unpredictability, his showing up whenever he felt like it, his not showing up whenever he felt like it. And I told her I was also exhausted by my own behavior. Because what I began to realize is that my manipulation, my control, my attempts to make him feel guilty, they were all driving him further away. It was driving him further away and was bringing them closer together. She became his safe place, the only person he could turn to.

My judgment of him, and my judgment of her, deepened their connection.

She began seeing me as the enemy. He began seeing me as the enemy. And I became the enemy. It became a constant battle, a battle with them and a battle within myself.

chapter 11 | waiting on god

You say you want peace,
do you lead with peace?

You say you want love,
are you being love?

You say you want it all,
do you know you're worthy of it all?

You can want all you want but . . .

God responds to your frequency,
your beingness,
your faith,
your trust,
your knowing,
your beliefs,
your conviction.

His wants and your wants are one and the same.
God wants what you want, that's a simple truth.

But are you aligned with what you say you want?

Do your words align with what you want?
Do your actions align with what you want?

Or are you waiting for something or someone else to go first?

Are you waiting on God . . .
 . . . waiting to have certainty.
 . . . waiting for the evidence.

It doesn't work that way.
God responds to you.

You and your commands.
You and your unwavering conviction.
You and your frequency.

GOD
RESPONDS
TO YOUR
FREQUENCY,
NOT YOUR
WANTS.

chapter 12 | spiraling down

We were on a never-ending roller coaster: the twists, the turns, the highs, the lows. I had no control over anything. How was I supposed to navigate this? How was I supposed to move forward? I was at Craig's mercy. He was popping in and out of our life when he wanted to see our son, and I never felt like it was enough. I wondered how it could be enough for him. How did he go from our son being his whole world to seeing him twice a week?

I judged him when he was there. I judged him when he wasn't there. It was a vicious cycle. I was constantly angry that our son didn't appear to be his number one priority. There was so much tension between us, and the next few months were not pretty.

At this point, I was focusing on him, so I didn't have to focus on me. So I didn't have to turn inward; so I didn't have to see my part in this; so I didn't have to look in the mirror.

Every time I started to feel something shift, something also exploded. And I realized I had to start looking at myself. It wasn't just him. My attempts to manipulate things, my attempts to control the situation, my attempts to force the ending of their relationship were all sending us into a darker hole.

During the days, I often felt like I had it together. I had my moments of choosing self-righteousness, but mostly I felt like I was handling this experience better than most would, definitely better than I would have if I wasn't pregnant.

I continued to have moments of knowing our story wasn't over, but it all felt so messy so much of the time, and there was so much fear living within me. This was most evident at night. At night, all my fears came to the surface.

Every night, at 4 a.m., like clockwork, my eyes would pop wide open, my body would jolt awake, and I'd feel a crushing weight on my chest. My heart would pound, and it felt like it was going to burst. It was hard to catch my breath. I anticipated what I knew was coming next. I'd try to stop it, but I couldn't. I'd try to will my way back to sleep, but it never worked. Questions about them rolled in so fast:

Where was he?
What were they doing?
What were they talking about?
How did this happen?
Why won't he talk to me?
When did everything start spinning so out of control?
Was he ever coming home?

Then, my fears for the baby girl growing inside me would surface. I couldn't imagine that these nightly experiences at 4 a.m. were good for her. At this point, I had received test results back that indicated there were some health concerns with my pregnancy.

She was only getting half the nutrients she was meant to due to a single-vessel umbilical cord. They wanted me to do further testing about a possible heart, kidney, or lung condition, and even though everything looked good from those tests, they told me to expect that at twenty-eight weeks, I may need to be induced because she may have a better chance of thriving outside versus inside of me. They said once I hit the twenty-eight-week mark in my pregnancy, I would need to be closely monitored every week and that every week after twenty-eight weeks I was still pregnant should be considered a gift.

It felt like our baby girl had an exit plan . . . just in case I couldn't get myself together.

There were the fears for her physical health, and beyond that, I also held so much fear about her future and how she would feel growing up knowing her dad abandoned her before they even met.

I also had fears about what my future would look like. It felt scary to not know what was coming next—to have zero idea of what my future held, our future held, my kids' futures held, our family's future held. Yes, I continued to feel it energetically that I was going to be okay, we were going to be okay, my kids would be okay. But what did okay even mean? I had dreams of taking our kids and living on the beach. I had the desire to drive west and move to the mountains.

Would that even be possible now?

What if Craig didn't let me move? What if I was forced to live a life in a city I no longer wanted to live in and felt like the exact opposite of what I wanted and what my soul craved?

I remembered the experience of a cousin who desperately wanted to move back to her hometown to be close to her family and her support system after she got divorced, but her ex wouldn't allow it. Would that be my story too? And then the next level of fear would kick in. How could I even afford to live in the city and provide a good life for my kids? Would his family, who had the money to pay for lawyers (and good ones), have some sort of control over my life? Was I free to even choose anymore?

I didn't know. I didn't have the answers.

This is when my head would take over and I'd let myself spiral down into all the worst-case scenario possibilities. The knowing and the not knowing at the same time was the worst. Knowing at the soul level that our daughter would be okay, we would be okay. But fearing at the human level she would not be, we would not be. Knowing at a soul level that our story, mine and Craig's, wasn't over, but fearing that it could be and having all the evidence stacked against me.

This almost destroyed me.

Not the not knowing itself, but the energy I spent trying to figure it out. The manipulation tactics I employed to try and control it. I wanted so desperately to find certainty in the uncertainty instead of surrendering to the uncertainty itself. I wasn't sure how to surrender to the uncertainty, but I started to dabble in it. I started to question my thoughts.

What if I was wrong?
What if it didn't need to be this way?
What if I wasn't the victim?
What if I could choose to do exactly what I wanted?
What if I was free from this marriage, this city, his family?
What if I was financially supported?
What if there were things I couldn't see yet?
What if more was being revealed to me?
What if I wasn't supposed to know?
What if the knowing or the need to know was the very thing that was creating the limitation?

I started to believe that God wouldn't put me in a situation where thriving wasn't available. And it felt like the baby girl growing inside of me was giving me signs. I felt her communicating with me, telling me, "Mama, I'm going to be okay." In my soul, I knew this to be true.

I was also willing to do everything at a human level to ensure this was so. That's what fueled the spiritual deep dive, the reading, the multiple times spent in meditation each day, the writing, the deep soul sessions, the hours upon hours spent with my energy healer. I wasn't willing to risk my baby's life, and it felt like that's what I would be choosing if I didn't find ways to calm my nervous system and shift my anger.

I began to love myself in ways I never had before. I connected with God, although at the time, "God" wasn't the word I chose to use. I trusted in the wisdom I sourced from within me, and I began to sit in sacred witness of myself. Witnessing where my human mind would try to take over, where I tried to protect myself, the stories I would make up, the untruths I would allow to enter, the fear that I had been allowing to lead.

chapter 13 | a woman of god would never

What I haven't shared with you yet is that a couple weeks prior to this experience that changed my life, I was sitting on my couch, looking out the window, when this thought entered my mind—more like it invaded my body: "There has to be more."

As quickly as the thought entered, I invited it to exit. Why did I want more? How could I want more? I had my precious almost two-year-old son. I had my long-awaited baby number two on the way. I was wildly in love with the man I married. I had a thriving business helping women who inspired and motivated me that I worked part-time while being a full-time stay-at-home mom.

I was so happy. How could I want more?
It felt so uncomfortable, this desire to want more.

How could I?
I had more than most people I knew.
I was thriving in every way I had ever dreamt of.

But there were things I hadn't fully dared to dream of. I had never allowed myself to desire at a human level what I could feel my soul craving. A soul-led life.

Sure, I had toe-dipped in spiritual curiosity throughout most of my life. I would say I believed in a higher power and that there was magic in the universe. I had connected to God in an on-and-off way, in the angelic realm, and via prayer. I had witnessed a miracle healing of my aunt's cancer. I had known for many years God was right there calling me. But for many years, I bounced back and forth between opening the door and slamming the door in God's face. Who was I to think I could have this type of connection with the divine?

At this point in my life, the only examples I had of soul-led humans were devout Catholic women and monks. You might think I'm joking, but I'm not. I was raised in a Catholic family, and traveling to Indonesia and Asia in my early twenties brought me into connection with monks. I looked at myself in the mirror and knew I definitely didn't match the definition of holy. I was a wild child, a party girl. And even though I left the church at twelve years old, not believing that sins exist in the way I was taught, I still felt that I was a sinner. I started drinking and having sex at fifteen—definitely not holy. I made a lot of, let's say, not-up-to-par choices in my teenage years and twenties. I have a list of people who could share many stories with you that would make you feel like I'm an impostor. Like "Wait, she did what? She did that?" A woman of God would never.

Well, let me tell you this. A woman of God would when she forgets she is a woman of God. When she hasn't allowed herself to tap into her divine nature, when she feels unworthy and undeserving of love—at a conscious or subconscious level—when she fears love, when she stops believing love even exists. This was me. I believed love was a fairy tale that didn't exist. I believed that love was a Hallmark card, a meaningless piece of paper easily thrown away. I had seen enough betrayal and infidelity around me and been hit on by enough married men to believe that most people cheat and love doesn't truly exist.

So, I turned away from love.
And turned away from God.

Better not to want, better to shut it off, better not to desire it if the desire isn't possible. Right?

And this is why, on our third date, I told Craig I didn't believe in love and didn't ever want to get married. Clearly marking the lines and putting those protective barriers in place. But as we know, he broke through. I surrendered to love existing, but this love was still limited because this love was a love I experienced outside of me. Incredible in so many ways, but there was always this underlying feeling that this love could be taken away. Not because the love wasn't real and true, as I had previously feared, but because I didn't feel I was the source of love.

I hadn't yet realized that I am love.
You are love.
God is love.

And we are here to express that which we truly are, LOVE.
That realization came later on.

chapter 14 | divine love

Many of us have not been on the receiving end of love that is unconditional. And therefore, we don't know how to believe in love that is unconditional. But this is what we are here to experience. Divine Love, that is pure and true.

This divine love is experienced within first. When you come into connection with the God within, the divine within, the universe within. When you step into the remembrance of what your soul already knows:

You are heaven in human form.
You and God are one and the same.

God does not reside outside of you, she is not a higher power, he is not the miracle worker.
She is not the answer to your prayers.

You are.
You are the creator, the lover, the miracle worker, the one.
You are the purest expression of love.
You are the truth.
You are the answer to your prayers and their prayers.
You are the way.
You are the Goddess.

chapter 15 | queen of my kingdom

I started to seriously explore the idea that this was happening for me. And not from the surface-level belief I had before of "everything happens for a reason," which I kind of believed, but kind of didn't.

I started to ask myself in each moment, with each thought, with each experience: "If this is happening for me, then what? Where am I being called to grow? What level of awareness am I being called to step into?"

I started to call this experience of life my Spiritual Smackdown and decided it would be the experience that fully awakened me. After all, it felt like God no-optioned me.

That feeling I had right before "that there was something more." The fact that I was pregnant and needed to find alternative ways to respond—I couldn't simply rage with alcohol, sex, and partying.

God was answering a prayer I didn't even know I had asked.

From the beginning, since the day I found out, I said I didn't think Craig's affair was about me. I couldn't have been more wrong. While Craig's affair might not have been about us, while it didn't feel like a reflection of his feelings for me or our marriage, it did have everything to do with me.

It was about my journey, my spiritual awakening, and about Craig's journey too; it was about my journey to love and his journey to love.

Like always, when these thoughts came flooding to me, I reached for my journal. I wanted to get these thoughts out on paper so I could come back and read them whenever I felt lost.

This is what I know.

Craig is on his own journey. I am on my own journey.

I am on a journey, awakening my spirit, and I have all I need within me. I have let go of my past. I am learning from the lessons, but I have no desire to return here. I am okay with the unknown. I have faith. I trust in the divine plan and the divine guidance the universe has mapped out for me.

I show my children strength and resilience. We live an unconventional life. We are spiritual beings; we wander, we travel, we adventure. I teach them about love, God, angels, life. And they teach me.

I am LOVE.

I am one with God and my angels. I am fulfilling my higher purpose. I am teaching and leading the women of the world. I am sunshine, I am happy. My days are filled with joy, abundance, and laughter. I live with simplicity. I live in nature with my family. Lots of green, lots of water, lots of warmth, sun, ocean, sand, fresh foods.

Craig is on his own journey and has his own lessons to learn. I cannot control this. I cannot try to speed this up. All I can do is send him love, be patient, and detach myself from the drama and his current situation.

Where Craig is at right now is not the man I married. He is not what

I want for me or my children. His actions are not a reflection of me or his feelings toward me or our kids.

Craig will come to a fork in the road. He has the choice to join us on this journey, to rise and be the man and father we deserve. He must choose, though; it is his free will. God knows I pray he chooses the path back to his family, to join us on our journey, to grow spiritually together. To choose this path, his family, he must be willing to turn inside, to deal with his past, to talk to me. We can support him on his journey and welcome him with open arms, but he needs to do the work. We deserve nothing less.

We love him. We will wait but also move forward.

Craig is doing the best he can in this moment. His best is not enough for us long term, but he has the power to CHOOSE . . . to face his fears and his emotions, and to overcome them. In the meantime, I create my castle as I commit to being the Queen of my Kingdom!

I knew I needed to keep going with that feeling. The feelings that this Spiritual Smackdown was happening for me not to me. It felt like the catalyst I needed to put the spark back in my soul. It's what I needed to stop feeling like I was a victim. It's what I needed to unleash the Goddess within me.

As this awareness became clearer, I sat down to email my girls . . . the ones in the know.

I really need to stop focusing on Craig and his drama so I can step into my power. I feel like I can use this experience to catapult me to the next level, but I can only do that if I stop engaging in and stop reliving all the drama day after day. So, while I know you are all there for me, I just really need to stop talking about Craig, I need to ask you to stop sending me Instagram pictures of him and her . . . I know it's so addicting because it's better than reality TV, but I need your support in helping me rise above this, and my focus needs to shift to me, my babes, my biz, and my life!

And I promise if I need anything or a day to vent about how much this sucks, I will reach out . . . but being constantly asked how I'm doing, how I'm surviving, what's going on, etc. (even though I know it's with the best intentions), is leaving me stuck in "victim mode" that I need to escape!

Today, I am feeling excited about the next step in my journey!

xoxo

And thus, the journey *from Victim to Goddess* began.

GOD

GODS

FROM

WITHIN

YOU.

chapter 16 | I am because I am

"I am because I am" creates a knowing of who we are. To know ourselves as something different, we must be willing to leave behind our current level of knowingness: what we know to be true in this moment.

It's not required to make the leap into this new identity immediately. That's actually where people most often get lost and overwhelmed. The fact that I no longer choose to be the victim does not automatically make me the Goddess. It's a path: *from Victim to Goddess*.

So often, because we don't identify as the Goddess (yet), we fall back into the victim role again and again and again. We don't realize we are a Goddess in training, so we then shame and judge ourselves for having thoughts as a victim would. And so, the cycle continues.

Now to be clear, when I say it's a journey you embark on to become the Goddess, this is a journey you take within yourself. Of course, you already are the Goddess, because you are all that is. This is the journey into the remembrance that you are.

You are the Goddess.
You are the Divine.

chapter 17 | punishing them

I couldn't fully shake the victim mode. It felt like I'd take one step forward and then two steps back. Some days Craig showed up for our son, and some days he didn't. Some days I trusted we were going to get through this, and some days I felt like I was drowning.

Some days I felt like a Goddess, some days I felt like a victim.

This is where he had the power. His actions, or lack thereof, penetrated me so deeply. When he bailed on plans to see our son, an anger boiled up within me that I couldn't seem to control. An instant rage switch would get turned on. I didn't even recognize myself in those moments. I'd go from calm—I got this, we're going to be okay—to wanting to make him pay.

In those moments, I wanted revenge.
I wanted him to feel guilty.

I blamed him.
I criticized him.
I tore him apart.

I wanted to hurt him. I wanted him to feel a fraction of the pain I felt. And the next time he played games with me, I wanted him to know it.

At this point, Craig had blocked me from his phone, meaning I had no efficient way to get in contact with him, the father of my children, outside of emails. But the thing is, I wasn't supposed to know I was blocked from his phone; he hadn't told me yet, but I had been monitoring his emails and bank statements that I had access to on our computer. I read the correspondence between him and her,

I saw the dinner reservations he made. I knew exactly what he was up to, and I could track his every move.

It gave me a thrill to imagine I could have shown up in his new world at any time and it would all have gone crashing down hard and fast. So, on the day I saw an email from her to him that asked if I'd realized I'd been blocked, I decided I was going to give them a taste of their own medicine.

All day, I laid the groundwork.

I sent him a text asking him if he could come earlier for his night with our son, telling him I had dinner plans at 6 p.m. I called him several times, knowing the calls wouldn't go through. I texted him several times, knowing he wouldn't receive the messages.

And when he didn't show up by 5:50 p.m., I left after sending him a text that told him I took Kane with me to my dinner and he could pick him up there.

At 6 p.m., my phone rang. Craig was on the other end, asking where we were. "Didn't you get my texts?" I asked innocently. I told him I had been calling and texting him all day to confirm, but I didn't hear back from him and didn't know what to do.

I could feel him getting uncomfortable. I assume when they planned it, they thought blocking me was a game, it was punishment, and he would show me. But how was he supposed to explain this to me? He didn't even try, he just asked where we were and said he would be there in two minutes.

We hung up and I sent him a text that said sorry along with screenshots of the missed calls and texts, proving that I had tried my hardest to communicate with him all day.

Two minutes went by. Five minutes went by. Ten minutes went by. And then I got an email from him. His anger had kicked back in, and I could tell he had talked to her. His email said he couldn't keep operating with me like this. He told me he had blocked me from his phone and he wasn't coming to get Kane.

My plan backfired once again.

chapter 18 | becoming the villain

Throughout this Spiritual Smackdown, I had very vivid dreams. Most of them didn't make logical sense, but there seemed to be a deeper meaning in each one, something I was meant to take from them. It felt like God's way of communicating with me.

The recurring dream at this time had to do with selling our house. In the dream, Craig and I had agreed to host an open house together. I'm showing people around the house when I see Craig and Hannah coming down the stairs. What's she doing here? I did not agree to this and I'm pissed that he would think this is okay. In the dream, I get aggressive. I try to physically attack her, but I'm held back, so instead, I grab an egg off the kitchen counter and throw it at her. I miss, but that doesn't stop me. I grab another one, and this time, I don't risk missing. I walk straight up to her and crack it over her pretty blonde head. Then, Craig picks up an egg. I expect him to retaliate and throw it at me, but he doesn't. He surprises me by cracking it over his own head. He and Hannah are now both covered in egg, which somehow connects them. They are laughing, singing, and dancing. I'm the one left out. I'm the one who feels hurt and embarrassed in this situation. I want to run away and cry, but instead, I surrender. I give up the fight, I give up the struggle, and I apologize to her. They don't seem to care; they aren't mad at me. In fact, we all laugh about it and I end up dancing with them.

I woke up feeling like I betrayed myself in the dream because the human part of me didn't want that. I didn't want to dance with them, I didn't want to say sorry, I didn't want to give up the fight.

I tried to resist here, but the egg dream was glaring right in my face, showing me just how clear it was that my actions always, always, always created reactions. When my actions were unloving and fear-based, it took me further away from my desires and only hurt me.

I saw the sword I was repeatedly slicing over on my own head. I saw it, I understood what God was showing me, and yet I wasn't ready to surrender. I wasn't ready to shift from fear. I wasn't ready to choose love. I wanted to keep fighting; I still needed them to be the villains because I didn't know any other way to get what I wanted. I thought the only way for my family to come back together would be if I made it happen. If I could get Craig to see what I saw, if I could convince him. I needed to control the narrative to feel certain about the outcome.

But it was within this need to control it all that I pushed the thing I wanted most further away. My control created roadblocks for all of us.

chapter 19 | the illusion of control

As humans, we have this deep need to know. We have this deep need to want to be certain.

Why is this felt so strongly? Why do we have the deep need to control and protect ourselves from uncertainty?

Because if not, we might experience something that doesn't feel good. We might experience loss, we might experience heartbreak, we might experience pain, we might experience failure, we might be disappointed.

And in the desire to make it so certain that we're not going to experience loss, heartbreak, pain, failure, and disappointment, we block ourselves because we then try to control every aspect of everything we experience.

The illusion of control creates the illusion of certainty through this lens.

But here's the truth: it's an illusion that you're ever in control.
And you're also always in control.
This is part of the Divine dichotomy.

You're in control of your response to what is happening at any given moment, in any given experience you find yourself in.

You are not in control of the experience itself.

You're always in control of what thoughts you let live in your energy field.

You're always in control of whether you let fear stop you, limit you, or expand you.

You're always in control of your actions.
You're always in control of your choices.

This expression of control is not limiting. It's control without controlling, without force, without attachment, without need or lack.

But often, this is not the frequency of control we emit.

We try to control the outcome,
the timeline,
the how,
the who,
the when.

And honestly, we try not only to control the outcome but also all the little steps along the way. We try to control what people think, feel, say, do, experience.

And this is not in our soul's nature.

It's not in your soul's nature to operate under the confines of control. Because where there is control, there is resistance.

It works against the frequency of allowance, and allowance is the frequency of God.
Allowance rooted in faith and trust.

In certainty within the uncertainty.

chapter 20 | the tidal wave

After the day he told me he blocked me from his phone, I woke up to an email that said the only way Craig would communicate with me going forward was via email and that he would be at our house to pick up Kane at 5 p.m. I better be there, Kane better be ready, and he better have an overnight bag packed.

Over my dead body.

In that instant, I knew Craig planned on taking Kane to Hannah's house. This was my payback. This was the one thing we'd both agreed to: Kane was not allowed to meet Hannah until we had an agreement in place with our lawyers, and he definitely was not allowed to take him to her house. There was no f*cking way I was about to let that happen.

I wrote him back: "We need to talk before you come."

"There is nothing to talk about. Just have him ready."

I needed space and time to think, so I decided to take Kane over to my girlfriend's house. I called her as we were driving there so we could discuss my dilemma. Should I wait to talk to Craig when he came at five? Not a great idea because I knew this talk would be a blowout, and I didn't want Kane to be a witness to it.

Should I just go to my family's place for the weekend and not let Craig see Kane?

Should I go to his work and hash it out with him? This felt like my best move. He reacted differently when we were face-to-face. When he saw me, he couldn't keep tricking himself into believing I was the enemy. And if we kept communicating through email, it was going to be an all-out war.

I wanted to see him, to confront him, to make it clear to him that Kane would not be going anywhere unless Craig still agreed to follow our rules. I decided this was my plan, but my girlfriend tried to talk me out of it. She knew me showing up at his work would create more turbulence. It's like a reality show. One minute, things are running smoothly, then the next, we're at war.

She and I kept going back and forth. She knew I was too stubborn to listen to her, and as it turns out, I didn't have to. I pulled up in front of her house, and there on the side of the street, I saw Craig's truck. Weird! He should have been at work; it's the middle of the day. I think, *He must be here to see Hannah; she works around the corner.*

I wondered if I manifested it. I was talking to my girlfriend and telling her about the previous night's blowout, telling her I needed to see Craig before I felt comfortable handing Kane off for the night, and then there he was, right in front of me. I went to get out of the car to talk to him, and he drove away. I was now officially pissed. I knew he saw me, he knew I wanted to talk, and he was avoiding me. I lost my sanity; I got back in my car and took off after him.

My girlfriend was still on the phone, pleading with me to pull over, pleading with me to stop, but I hung up on her. I knew she was right, but I didn't want to listen; I didn't want to be the one who was continually holding it together. I wanted to let it all out.

Everything had been bottled up inside me for the past two months, and in this moment, I wanted Craig to understand what he had done.

I wanted to have a moment of choosing self-righteousness. I wanted to dwell in victim mode.

He pulled over down the street, we both got out of our cars, and there, in the middle of the street, we had it out. *This is it*, I think; *this is the worst it gets.* And then I spot it: a new tattoo on the inside of his ring finger.

With a smile on his face, he told me it said HL, her initials, and she had a matching one with CS.

I wanted to smack the grin right off his face. Seriously, I don't think I've ever felt rage like it. It was my breaking point. Somehow, this was the moment it all started to feel real. The tattoo represented something to me; the tattoo made me feel like there was no going back. This was permanent; his relationship was permanent, just like the ink on his finger.

"What the f*ck is wrong with you?" I screamed.

People stopped to stare at the crazy girl, but I didn't care. I continued screaming. "You can't just run around and get a tattoo of some chick's name on your finger, a chick you have known for two months."

He raged right back: "I can do whatever I want. You don't control me."

"Actually, you can't just do whatever you want! You have a pregnant wife and a two-year-old child."

He then had the audacity to say, "I never made a commitment to you."

Was he kidding me? "What do you think marriage is? It's a *commitment.*"

In this moment, I said all the things I had wanted to say for the past two months, everything I had been holding in, all of my thoughts about Hannah and his relationship. I asked him where the man I married went. I told him I thought he was a selfish asshole. I asked him what happened to the kind, loving man I'd married. The man who would do anything for anyone, the man who valued family, the man who honored and loved his wife.

He just laughed and told me I was crazy. Then he walked away and into his doctor's office, which meant I could no longer follow him. But I would be lying if I said I didn't want to. The only thing that was stopping me was the fact that Kane was still in the car.

I knew the sane thing at this point would have been for me to get in my car and drive away, but I didn't. I couldn't. I couldn't let him get away with this. So, I called my girlfriend back and asked her to come and get Kane. Again, she tried to convince me to leave, but I refused and begged her to just come and get him. I didn't know what would happen when Craig came back out, but I knew I didn't want our child to witness it. So, she did what I asked. She came and got him, and I sat on the side of the street and waited for Craig.

I knew I was giving him exactly what he wanted. He wanted me to lose my mind; it justified his actions. Who would blame him for walking away from his crazy wife? Every part of me knew I should leave, but I couldn't bring myself to do it. I waited until he was done at his appointment, and when he came out, I started walking toward him, but he walked right past me, got into his truck, and drove off.

Once again, I had the opportunity to walk away, but I wasn't done. This was not how this conversation was going to end, so I followed him.

We got into a car chase, a chase that crossed the city. It wasn't sane. We were both running red lights and driving the wrong way down one-way streets. Horns blared at us, but neither of us stopped. I finally caught up to him and trapped him, blocking him in with my car so that there was nowhere to go unless he left his truck and went on foot. For some reason, I thought forcing him to talk to me would result in a desirable outcome for me. It didn't, not in this energy. It made things a hundred times worse.

At the beginning of the day, I'd been blocked from his phone, worried that he was going to introduce our son to his girlfriend. And by the end of this conversation, he told me he wanted me to leave the city. He thought I should move away, and he didn't care to ever see me again. He said he planned to move away too.

Another screaming match on the side of the street ensued. *This is it*, I think. *He's truly going to do it. He's going to walk away from his kids.* She had become the most important person in his life; she's the one he would do anything for. And as if on cue, she called. He picked up and told her just how crazy I was.

F*ck this sh*t.

He didn't need to tell her how crazy I was, I would let her experience it for herself. I reached out and grabbed the phone from him. Surprisingly, he didn't put up a fight. He let me take it. And there, for the first time, I heard her voice; there, for the first time, I was ready to confront the woman who stole my husband.

The conversation started out pretty viciously. She told me how crazy she thought I was, told me to get a job and support myself, to stop depending on Craig, to accept that we were getting divorced. Oh, and she told me to get a life of my own.

I told her I had a f*cking life until she came along. I told her we were happy until she entered the picture. I told her how crazy I would get and asked her if she really wanted to deal with me for the next twenty years.

We were both yelling at each other and then, it all just stopped when she said, "You know, I'm not chaining him to my bed. He is free to leave anytime he wants. If that's what he wants, he can go back to you."

And from there, we started to talk. She told me that their life together wasn't what I thought it was; it wasn't just parties, sex, and good times. It was hard. She said there were many nights Craig would cry himself to sleep, not sure how to handle the pain he had caused and the pain he felt. She said nights were the hardest for him when he wasn't seeing Kane.

She said yes, they had talked about moving away to get away from me, but she knew he never actually could. She told me what I already knew: that in the beginning, she hadn't known I was pregnant and then once she found out, she was already in too deep. She also confirmed that I found out about the affair pretty much the moment it began, and she told me she really believed Craig had been unhappy in our marriage for a while.

It feels so weird to say this, but after talking to her for twenty minutes, I started to feel a shift of energy within me. It was close to the feeling of peace. I remembered that she's human, he's human, I'm human, and we're all a little f*cked up.

This is also when I realized that the three of us were living in a very intertwined situation and it was a situation we were each experiencing differently. We all saw through a different lens. I realized this, and I wanted to understand more. This is when temptation hit again, and again my soul said don't do it, but my human took over.

By this point, Craig and I were no longer on the same street. While Hannah and I were talking, I had gotten in my car and driven away, taking Craig's phone with me. And there it was, his phone, with all their communication, all the text messages they had exchanged. I pulled over on the side of the road and began to scroll through two months of their texts.

I immediately regretted it. I wanted to bleach my eyeballs and erase what I had read from his phone, from my memory, from the universe. Messages where he told her she was the most important person in his life, messages where he said he had never felt like this before, messages where he exclaimed that one specific day had been the best day of his life.

Messages where she told him I was manipulating him, messages where she said she would spit on me if she ever saw me on the street, messages where they discussed running away to Australia to start a new life and a new family across the world. And then I saw the messages that ultimately broke me. The ones where he told her about the complications with my pregnancy, and she said she knew it all along. He should have made me pee on a stick in front of him because she never thought I was pregnant to begin with.

That close-to-peace feeling I had just felt was instantly wiped away. She couldn't actually think that, could she? There was no way, but she did. As I continued to read their texts, I saw that she thought, or at least told him that she thought, that I faked my pregnancy, thought I was pretending to have complications so I could pretend to lose the fake baby and blame it all on Craig and the stress he caused me.

Now who was the crazy one? It's got to be her. He must tell her she's crazy; he must tell her he knows that I am pregnant; he must tell her about the genetic testing we had done and about the ultrasound he saw . . . but nope. As I continued to scroll down, I saw his responses to her, and he agreed. He said he thought I might be faking my pregnancy too.

I didn't scroll past that—that was enough for me. I took his phone and drove over to his work, intending to just give it back. I didn't have it in me to fight anymore, not after what I'd just read. I felt completely defeated, and I could tell he felt defeated too. He didn't have it in him to fight anymore either. I didn't want to fight, but I needed to know. There was one question I told him I had to ask:

"Do you actually think I'm not pregnant?"

He shrugged. "Well, you don't look pregnant."

My jaw dropped. I opened my mouth, but nothing came out. And then I turned and walked away, because there was no response to that. I went home and dug out a box from the back of my closet that had four ultrasound pictures and laid them on my bed. There was the one of Kane, the one of the baby boy we'd lost, the one of the baby girl we'd lost, and the last one of our daughter.

I snapped a picture, sent it to Craig, and then Kane and I left the city.

chapter 21 | it's not worth disrupting your peace

It's not worth disrupting your peace.

> That thought . . .
> that belief code . . .
> that action . . .
> that pattern . . .

Not worth it. They are not worth disrupting your peace. The "they" in your head that don't really exist. The "they" from your past, the ones that you fear are judging you. The "they" from your present, the ones who are actually judging you. Not worth it.

When your peace is disrupted, it's a sign that something is off.

Sure, you can go into fix-it mode, you can dissect it, analyze it, overthink it. You can also choose something different. You can choose a new thought, a new belief code, a new action, a new non-action. Whatever aligns with you protecting your peace. It's all a choice. You choose peace, love, happiness . . . and you choose fear, frustration, anger, control.

This is where you're in control.

And not control that is rooted in illusion.
Not control from force, or manipulation.

But you in control of your divine remembrance.
You in control of what you let live in your energy field.
You in control of paving new energetic pathways.

You're painting the canvas, so paint it all. Don't shame your human, then choose. Choose what to highlight, choose what you focus on, choose what you bring forward. And harness your personal power so that "it" and "they" don't disrupt your peace.

chapter 22 | I need to know

"This has to be it. I get to be done now . . . right? I get to stop loving Craig, don't I? God, please tell me I get to end all this now."

These were the words I prayed as we drove out of town. I prayed for God to show me. I prayed for him to give me a sign that what I felt in my soul wasn't true.

The human part of me that no longer wanted to suffer wanted to tell me that this was the end of us. My husband had another woman's name tattooed on his ring finger, so of course this had to be where the story ends. But there continued to be this other part of me that said our story wasn't over. And so, I prayed to God, to my angels, to the universe, to anyone out there in the spirit realm that might be able to help me, I prayed to be shown.

And what I was shown was this. God is limitless and love is limitless. I was shown that just when we think we can't possibly go any further, just when we think we are at our limit, that is when the breakthrough can occur, that's when we are shown just how limitless we are.

This is what I was shown through the eyes of my soul, but I asked for human confirmation. I had yet to learn to completely trust my soul. So, I asked for confirmation in the form of signs, asking for three signs to guide me, three signs that would give me the answer I was so desperately searching for.

Immediately and out of nowhere, I reached out my hand to change the radio station I had been listening to—the radio station I always listened to—but for some reason on this day, on this drive, I wanted to find a new station. I felt paralyzed for a moment when the station

I flipped to was playing our wedding song, and our version of our wedding song, a song I had only ever heard played at our wedding, definitely not on the radio.

This had to be a fluke. I told myself it didn't mean anything, but I also tracked the score. One sign calculated toward our story wasn't over.

And then moments later, I heard Kane's voice from the backseat. "Mommy, look what I found." He was holding a small silver coin. On one side there was a picture of an angel, and on the other side, an engraving of the word "hope."

I continued to drive, tears streaming down my face, surrendering. I heard God speak loud and clear, confirming what I already knew. This part of our journey, the story of us, was far from over.

But why was it so hard, I questioned. Why did it seem like Craig and I kept banging against a steel wall? When was this going to end?

I didn't even need the third sign, but I got it. Kane had fallen asleep in his car seat, and while he was sleeping, his sweet little voice whispered, "Daddy loves Mommy."

chapter 23 | his soul-knowing

A few days went by, the aftermath of the tidal wave was beginning to fade, and this is when something clicked in me: If Craig was so sure of what he was doing, if he was truly committed to his decisions, if he believed Hannah was his future, why was he hiding it?

Why hadn't he told the people at his work? Why did his friends only know because I'd told them?

Why wasn't he pushing for his family to meet her? Why wasn't he pushing for our son to meet her? Why, if he was so sure, was he keeping his relationship in the dark? I didn't think it was intentional, but I thought maybe there was something underlying in him. Maybe his soul knew what my soul knew: that this wasn't how our story was going to end.

chapter 24 | the tidal wave dream

It was a week after the car chase that I had the tidal wave dream for the first time. I saw the first part of the dream, the part when I was walking down the beach as the tidal wave hit, as a heads-up from God, not meant to instill fear, but more like "Hey, Jak, another tidal wave is coming; be prepared."

I had not responded well to the last tidal wave, but I would be getting another chance. Another chance to find my center, another chance to rise in my power, another chance to see through the eyes of God and to choose peace.

And the second part of the dream, the part when I was in the glass room, showed me that I could choose to see the beauty in the chaos. If I sat calmly, in sacred witness, the tidal wave couldn't control me. I could choose to react the same way I did when the first tidal wave hit, when I'd spotted Hannah's name tattooed on Craig's finger; I could let anger and fear consume me. I could run away from it and choose to see only the dark side. Or I could see it for what it was and embrace the beauty in it.

I reached out to one of my soul sisters to tell her about this dream, knowing she would likely have some deeper insights into the meaning of it. She felt I was receiving a message and direction from God to go inward. He was showing me that this would be a time of calm, a time to process, a time to write, a time to reflect on all that had happened. And it would also be a time to own my part in all of it. She said God was very clear in that I needed to take this time for me so I would be prepared when the next tidal wave hit. I felt this truth in every part of my being.

I armed myself with spiritual texts. Reading had become my sanctuary. I began to write daily. I started meditating, something I had been trying to do for years but never got it, and then I found myself meditating multiple times a day.

I didn't do this to check out but to check in.

I continued to go to restorative yoga. I found a new class with an extraordinary instructor who I loved. Each class, I felt a deep surrender and a deeper connection to the God within me. Then, a few nights after the tidal wave dream, I was in class, lying on my yoga mat, and the instructor invited us to ask the divine to guide us. She encouraged us to ask God a question and to be open to receiving an answer.

I never thought I could just ask God, or the divine, or the universe a direct question like that. I had asked the question before during my session with the psychic if Hannah would ever leave my marriage, but that was different. There was someone, a person acting as an intermediary between me and God. She was a spiritual translator who could give me an actual answer. I had asked my angels for signs before, but this—I wasn't sure I could actually do it. However, I'd developed a relationship with this teacher, and I trusted her, so I figured it couldn't do any harm.

So, as class began, I asked the universe if I was supposed to keep fighting or if I was supposed to give up hope, to accept that my marriage was over, and to move on.

I didn't understand how I was supposed to get this answer. I thought maybe I would feel something in my body release and that would be some sort of indicator to me that I was supposed to release Craig, but that didn't happen. It felt like nothing happened. Then, at the end of class, while everyone was lying in savasana, the teacher picked up a book and read us a prayer.

It was the most beautiful prayer I had ever heard, not at all like the prayers I used to have to recite at church. The prayer was called "Honoring Ebb and Flow" by Pixie Lighthorse. And the part I focused on was when she spoke of dangerous waves that threaten our existence, yet God teaches us to ride them effortlessly. Our right path will appear before us when we surrender and put in our best efforts.

More waves, more waves threatening to take me out. There was an obvious theme between this prayer, my dream, and my friend's message. It felt clear that another tidal wave was headed my way. And it was clear that the assignment was to remember that I get to choose. I could choose love, I could choose peace, I could choose to see the beauty in the storm.

I could choose to let the tidal wave roll over me and experience peace, or I could let fear take over—and then the wave would take me down, again.

chapter 25 | the shift

When you no longer choose to be one thing, this is when you are meant to sit in sacred witness of yourself, in a state of being, allowing yourself to sit in conscious awareness of your current thought patterns and judgments of self and to see the untruths in each.

Awareness is the key here.

Becoming so aware of the thoughts, fears, and stories you hold that have created who you are in this moment—and then consciously choosing to release those beliefs. I call these "belief codes," things that have been subconsciously coded, or shall I say programmed, into your system that are running the show without your awareness (until you choose to become aware, that is) as you recognize you are truly not that.

Seeing that which you are not before seeing that which you are. Knowing I was not the victim opened me up to see who I truly am.

Knowing that I got to choose, knowing that I had the power within me—this is what shifted everything.

chapter 26 | sole custody

I didn't have to wait long for the second tidal wave to hit. Craig and I had an appointment scheduled with the family mediator. We'd both continued to see her individually, but this time she wanted us to meet together.

The intention of this session was not about him and me, it was to work out a plan for our kids; to figure out a way to move forward with their best interests at heart. We both committed to the appointment.

The night before, he'd been at our house to spend time with Kane, and as he left, he said he'd pick me up at 8 a.m. and we'd drive together. I don't know what happened between 10 p.m. and 8 a.m. (well, actually, I had a pretty good idea), but at 8 a.m., I got a message saying he wasn't coming.

So many parts of me wanted to explode. Rage flooded me, and I wanted to march over to her house and scream at him all over again. I didn't want to just accept it, but I did. I accepted that I couldn't control him, and I went to the appointment alone.

When I got there, our mediator told me that Craig had emailed her that morning saying he felt uncomfortable being in the same room as me. She said it didn't surprise her. She said the last time he was there, he walked into her office and said he was there to discuss Kane but didn't want to talk about his marriage at all.

She said, "He can't go there, he can't talk about you because it brings up feelings of remorse and guilt, and he doesn't want to deal with that pain inside him."

She said the last time they'd had a session together, it had been extremely emotional for him. "He can't let you see him like that. If he does, this whole new life he has created will crumble. He can't let his guard down."

She also told me I was "dealing with a very broken man."

She continued to tell me more about their sessions, reading from her notes, which surprised me. I thought it was against some sort of confidentiality code, but she assured me it wasn't because she was acting as a mediator between us. The things I shared with her could be shared with him, and the things he shared with her could be shared with me. This was news to me, and I'm sure it was unknown to Craig as well.

Honestly, it felt good to hear someone else seeing and saying the things I had been feeling about Craig and about us. She saw his patterns of avoidance, she saw the pain he was in, and she saw just how fragile his choices were.

She said he told her he wanted to be there for his kids, and she believed him. She said the pain she saw in his eyes when he talked about us was heartbreaking. She said they talked about his dad and how Craig viewed him for not being around during his childhood. He said he didn't want that for our kids. But she was worried he wouldn't know how to be there as a dad if he wasn't in our everyday lives. I had demanded that Kane and Hannah were to have no contact with each other, which was creating a lot of disruption in Craig's relationship.

She said he wouldn't be able to continue living these two separate lives, one that includes Kane and one that included Hannah. And as much as she believed Craig when he said he had no intention of abandoning his kids, she wanted me to be prepared for the worst.

That one day, Craig might walk away from us for good.

She grabbed my hand and squeezed it tight as she told me: "He wants you to have sole custody, and he said you're all better off without him."

My heart shattered all over the floor.

I spent the rest of the session in tears, and I spent the entire drive home in tears. Every time I felt like we were taking a step in the right direction, a step that would at least allow us to be at peace for our kids, it seemed like the next day we took two steps back. Again, I wondered if this was a sign from the universe telling me to give up, telling me my marriage was over and I needed to move on. It was the thing I was so desperate to know. I was so desperate to be able to see beyond what I could see in that moment.

So again, as I crawled into bed that night, I asked the universe for guidance; I asked and then I drifted off to sleep. This was the night the sex dream came back.

chapter 27 | sex dreams

It was 4 a.m., and my eyes shot wide open. My dream about Craig was so intense that I woke up, in real life, mid-orgasm.

What was going on? How could this be? I was so angry at him, and even though my soul knew our journey wasn't over, the rational part of my brain said that it was. So, why was I having another sex dream about him? It was the fifth time in the past three weeks.

The first time I had this dream, it took place in my childhood home. I was walking by the spare bedroom and saw Craig in the bed. I asked him what he was doing there. He said, "I told you I was coming by last night."

I didn't recall this, but I took a deep breath and lay down beside him. I didn't touch him, I didn't say anything, I just wondered how we got there. Almost immediately, the chemistry was there, and we ripped each other's clothes off. The sex was hot and deeply connected. I thought he had to be missing this, he couldn't possibly have this with someone else.

I woke up in a state of pleasure. The affirmation of our sexual connection felt so deeply woven that it reaffirmed my belief that our journey together wasn't over.

The second, the third, the fourth time I had this dream, the exact same scenario played out in the spare bedroom of my childhood home. However, in this dream, I came home to our house and Craig was lying on our couch.

I initially perched myself on the opposite end of the couch, but within seconds, I was aggressively pouncing on him. I was the initiator in this dream; in all the other dreams, he'd been the initiator. This time, he pulled away from me, saying it wasn't right, that he was with someone else. But it didn't stop me from pursuing him, and he couldn't deny me because our connection was so strong. We were having deep, intense, emotional, passionate sex in our living room, and this is when I woke up at 4 a.m. mid-orgasm.

It felt different this time. I no longer felt empowered by this dream; I no longer felt that it was an affirmation that our journey wasn't over. I felt like the "other woman," and I vowed to myself that I would never let that happen.

chapter 28 | a new perception

It was clear to see how my actions always caused a reaction. Every interaction Craig and I had, every email, every text, my response set the stage for what came next. I began to understand that as humans, our energy affects people in ways we can't even imagine.

Up until this point, a lot of my actions had been driven by fear. Fear, anger, control, and punishment had taken over my life. When I told Craig that Hannah wasn't going to be allowed to meet our kids until our daughter was four years old, I justified it to myself by claiming it would be best for our kids. They were so little, they would be so confused, it was all so unfair to them. But how could I ever have predicted, in that moment, what was going to be best for our kids six months, a year, four years from then? I was so focused on what our future would look like if Hannah was here to stay because it terrified me. I feared the worst.

I feared my kids liking her; I feared them not liking her. I worried about her liking them; I worried about her not liking them. I hated the thought that the four of them might get to do all the things together that I wanted the four of us to be doing. What if she really was the love of Craig's life? I pictured her sitting at my son's hockey games and them sitting together on the other side of the room at school plays, and I thought absolutely not. I wouldn't allow that to happen. I told myself, and Craig, there was no way this chick was going to be a role model in my daughter's life as clearly, she had no morals.

It's the fear that created all the anxiety within me, and I could see it taking its toll on Craig too. From his point of view, my insistence that Kane and Hannah were to have zero interaction was my way of punishing him. He wasn't wrong. I was on a mission to punish him and punish her. I wanted them to feel the pain I felt. As a result, Craig was constantly in a position to choose between Kane and Hannah. But it was me who continued to experience the pain. Every time he chose her over our son, it was me that felt the hurt, it was me who got so incredibly angry. Kane and Craig were fine. They would just pick up where they left off the next time they saw each other.

I sat on the sidelines, watching this play out time after time, until I was ready to acknowledge that my pain was self-inflicted, just like the egg dream foretold. My desire to punish, my desire for them to hurt, was setting this up. I was the one who kept putting Craig in a position to choose, knowing that he had already made his choice and had made it very clear. He had chosen her.

I knew I had to start taking radical responsibility for the part I was playing if I wanted the cycle to end. While I wasn't ready to fully surrender and wave the white flag, meaning I was still not ready to agree to Hannah meeting my child, I did stop trying to set him up to fail.

I stopped purposely putting him in situations where he had to choose. And when it happened naturally, like it did a few weeks later when he chose to go out of town with her instead of spending the weekend with Kane, I chose gratitude over anger and resentment.

Gratitude that I got to spend the time with Kane, gratitude that we could do whatever we wanted and go wherever we wanted, and gratitude that I didn't have to split my time with him 50/50, something I had never chosen.

This is also when I really began to look at the victim/villain part of the storyline that I had been so attached to. I started to look at the lens in which I viewed Craig through my human eyes, and I started to wonder what it would be like to look through a new lens.

I had been reading Marianne Williamson's book A *Return to Love* and there was a part where she talked about looking at life, looking at experiences, looking at people through the eyes of God.

I couldn't connect to that. The moment I would try to look through God's eyes, my mind would take over and say *But you aren't God. God is not here having the experience you are having, he doesn't see what you see, and you don't see what he sees.*

So, while looking through God's eyes did not feel accessible to me, there was something that did. I could look through Kane's eyes. I figured Kane's eyes were so pure, so full of love, so void of judgment that it must be pretty close to how God sees.

And so, I shifted. When Craig would show up at our door, I saw him as Kane saw him. I felt happy about the time they were about to spend together and stopped focusing on the time they didn't spend together.

I started viewing Craig through these childlike eyes, and I also started to remember he was once a child, which created another shift.

*IT'S EASY TO
LOOK THROUGH
OUR OWN LENS.*
WE CREATE UNITY
WHEN WE CAN LOOK
THROUGH THE LENS
OF OTHERS.

chapter 29 | self-righteousness

The moments I chose self-righteousness over peace were the moments when everything blew up. And that's a fact. The moments I chose their suffering over my peace. The moments I wanted him to pay. The moments I wanted her to pay—to pay for their actions, to pay for their choices. The moments I allowed fear to take over. The moments I tried to make him see what he was doing, what he was choosing was wrong. The moments I used shame as a tactic, criticism as a tactic, punishment as a tactic. These are the moments that brought them closer together and created more separation between us.

It created the dynamic of Me vs. Them. Victim vs. Villain.

This is when I noticed something interesting happening. This is when I started seeing our roles quickly being reversed. When I chose to sit in the seat of the victim, therefore placing them in the seats of the villains, the chairs would get flipped. They started to see themselves as the victims and me as the villain.

It felt like there was no escaping it. And from a human perspective, I would have to say that they were right. I wasn't acting as my truest self. I wasn't operating in the frequency of love. I was trying to inflict pain. I wanted them to hurt because I was hurt. I didn't see then that my love would be the antidote for all of us . . . that was coming up next.

That was the message God was trying to deliver, and every time I indulged and allowed myself to embark down the pathway of the victim, every time I ever even entertained the thought, God was there to intervene, showing me in my dreams or my physical reality what I was creating.

And inviting me to choose again.

WHAT IF
YOUR LOVE
IS THE
ANTIDOTE?

JOURNAL ENTRY

Today, there are so many "parts" of me. I am feeling frustrated, I am feeling inspired, I am feeling annoyed, I am feeling confused. I am in the dark, totally clueless to what happened, what you had been feeling leading up to all this. I don't think I will ever have answers to these questions.

I know right now the best thing I can do is focus on ME.

It's so hard to protect my energy from your actions. One day it is easy to have FAITH. Deep down I believe in "this or something better," but it's also so hard to watch you crumble like this, to see and feel the yo-yo effects of your emotions. All I want to do is lift you out of this mess, to convince you to talk to someone and get help. At this point, I am not asking you for anything for me or us. I want you to get your life together for our babies. Kane loves you so much!

I want you to get your life together for you! It's hard for me to navigate all this with Hannah involved. Yes, I am hurt; yes, I am angry; yes, I am jealous she's in your life. I'm trying so hard to let go of all these emotions, to stop judging her or you or your relationship. It is so difficult. One day I feel like I have this mastered, and the next I feel I'm at your mercy, like your words and actions have all the power over me.

What happens to set you up on these roller coasters?

The ocean of tidal waves is hard to navigate, and all I feel I can do is breathe deeply and deepen my connection with God and my angels, all while trying to stay calm through this storm. And I am trying, I am trying to stay in the present, but I am also anticipating the next tidal wave. I need to let this one roll over me.

JOURNAL ENTRY

Sometimes when I sit here and watch Kane like this, I get a pain in my heart—a good pain. I always knew I would love my children this much, but I had no idea I would love you this much and love you so deeply.

As much as I loved you on our wedding day, as much as I loved you the day before you left, I had no idea I could love you through this. We are LOVE . . . that's all any of us is filled with.

I recognize the love I have within me, I recognize the love I have to share, I recognize the power of this love.

And with these words, I started to feel gratitude toward Craig for igniting me on this journey.

IT'S SO SIMPLE WHEN YOU MOVE FROM YOUR SOUL.

IN BEFORE OUT.
SOUL KNOWING.
SOUL TRUTH.
DEEPER
BEFORE HIGHER.

chapter 30 | I want you to be happy

The next morning, I woke up to an email from Craig: "I think I cried myself to sleep last night. I miss him so much, he's just the best. I hate that I am not with him every day; he just makes me so happy. I would do anything for him. Please give him a big kiss for me this morning, and I can't wait to see him tomorrow."

This email tugged at my heart. It was one thing that Craig had decided he no longer wanted to be married to me, but I knew Kane was his whole world and I honestly didn't understand how he was surviving seeing Kane just a few hours a week.

I responded back to this email and shared a video of the two of them from a little over a year earlier when Kane was taking his first steps. We were at the park, together and happy. It felt like it was a lifetime ago. The smile Craig had in that video, the look in his eyes, the laugh . . . I wondered if I would ever see that side of him again. I wondered if he would ever see that side of himself again. It had been so long.

We ended up emailing back and forth a few times that morning, then he FaceTimed Kane midmorning, something that had never happened before. He'd been so committed to what he had previously told me: his time with Kane was his time with Kane, and when it wasn't his time, when he was at work or with her, there was no contact.

As soon as I picked up, I could see how much he was struggling with the distance between him and his child. Yes, he was the one that chose it, but I didn't want it to be like this. I never did. I didn't want Craig to have to wait until the next night, his scheduled time, to see his son. I wanted him to be able to pop by and see him every day if he wanted. I wanted them to have spontaneous dates to the park and for ice cream. I wanted them to be together; I wanted them to be happy. I wanted Craig to be happy, and I wanted to make peace with him. I wanted him to know that even though we were at war, it didn't need to affect his relationship with his son.

After the video call, Kane and I went for a bike ride, one of his favorite things to do. As we were biking through the park, he said, "We're going to Daddy's work?"

I was always so amazed at the things a two-year-old could remember. The summer before, we used to bike to visit Craig at work all the time, but it had been almost a year since we had done that. Still, if I wanted peace between us, maybe I needed to make the first peace offering, and I decided this would be a good idea. We could bike to Craig's work and Craig could give Kane that big kiss he wanted me to give him, himself.

I didn't think about how Craig would react. I knew Kane would be excited to see his daddy, and I knew my intentions were stemming from love. To show Craig love and to show him how much I appreciated him opening up to me that morning, showing me his vulnerable side.

The look on Craig's face when we biked up was one of incredible happiness. His whole face lit up as he scooped Kane up in his arms, giving him a million kisses. I told him we were just popping by for a quick kiss, but he asked if we could go for donuts, Kane's favorite treat. After the shock wore off, I said sure they could go. I planned to stay behind, but Craig turned and said, "Aren't you coming?" and just like that, off we went.

Craig was so excited to have Kane with him. He proudly introduced him to everyone who stopped to say hi. If you would have been sitting there watching us at the donut shop, you would have thought we were the most beautiful, happy family. You would have seen the three of us telling stories, you would have seen a father and son who couldn't take their eyes off each other, and you likely would have thought, "God, they are the lucky ones." And if you stuck around a little longer, you would have watched us get up to leave and you would have heard Craig ask us to sit back down and have one more donut together. You would have heard him say he didn't want to go back to reality, that he didn't want this moment to end.

I couldn't resist, so of course I said yes. The war between us was never something I wanted. So, we sat there for a few more moments, oblivious to the outside world. And then the time came for Craig to head back to work, so off we went again, Kane on Craig's shoulders, me and my bump walking beside them. We got back to Craig's work, back to our bikes, and as we were about to part ways, Craig turned to me and said a simple thank you.

"You don't know how much this means to me." Then he asked if we could do it more often, if we could pop by on our bikes, if he could see Kane in the in-between moments of his life. Of course, I responded, and I promised we would bike by later in the week.

Finally, the peace I had been wanting between us felt like it could exist. We could finally choose to end the war.

I am almost embarrassed to say that I was surprised that night when I got another email from him. He'd done a complete 180. I read and reread the email multiple times, wondering if he actually wrote it himself. It said he appreciated us stopping by, but it was also inappropriate. He said we needed to stick to the schedule of when he saw Kane and it was not okay for me, for us, to just stop by his work like we did. He said it made him uncomfortable and it was manipulative.

He went from such a high, begging us to stay longer, begging us to pop by his work more often, to telling me not to do it again within a matter of hours. It was the exact kind of moment I had been preparing myself for, a moment when I was invited to take a step back and drop into the remembrance that my reaction would dictate what happened next. It was the lesson I was continually learning. Craig was not ready to see my actions for what they were: actions of love, actions to build peace. It was easier for him, and easier for her, to see my actions as a ploy, as manipulation. This allowed them to continue seeing me as the villain.

He needed to learn to love himself before he could see that my actions stemmed from love. While his reaction in the moment was one of pure bliss, in the aftermath, he'd felt like he lost "control." When he allowed his emotions to take over it jeopardized his control, and that's what he was needing to shut down. He was so committed to proving to himself and everyone else that he was making the right choice. I wondered how long he would continue to choose being right over being happy.

God was giving me a sign here; a painful sign I was finally ready to see. Craig was not ready, he didn't see what I saw, and for him to keep living his life with her, the only thing he could choose was war with me. This was one of those moments when I reminded myself, again, that Craig was doing the best he could in this moment, and that his best was miles away from what I wanted.

It was time for me to fully surrender, to stop creating and controlling these situations. I needed to let go, to detach, and to have patience. I had to stop trying to speed up his awakening. I had to stop using Kane to open up Craig's heart; he needed to feel it and open it up himself. I couldn't force it. My job was to have faith, faith that he could and he would open his heart. I trusted that when he did, when he chose it himself, it would ultimately be more powerful.

I couldn't learn this lesson for him. That's not how it worked. He was on his own soul journey, and I was on mine. This journey was taking me to places I never would have imagined, causing me to re-think much of what I thought I knew, inviting me to know my truth and stand in my truth in ways I hadn't before.

I had my truth, and Craig had his. He could react based on his perception of the situation, but I knew my truth. I knew my actions stemmed from love and it was up to me to not allow his actions to control my emotions and my behaviors. I was the one responsible for creating my happiness, no one else.

From here, I decided to drop my expectations of Craig. I decided to drop my expectation of him wanting more: more time with Kane, more moments of love. Anything outside of what he was offering—his regular Tuesday, Thursday, and Saturday nights with Kane—was a bonus. By removing my expectations of what Craig should do and how Craig should feel, I was limiting my opportunity for disappointment.

The lesson for me came in strong: DETACH. DETACH. DETACH.

Detach from the outcome. Detach from my own expectations.

Another letter to him:

JOURNAL ENTRY

There is so much to process and release. I know I am strong enough;

I know I can do this. I am worthy of a beautiful life full of love. Our

kids are worthy of a beautiful life full of love. You are worthy of a beautiful life full of love . . . and we will keep on loving you. As hard

as it gets, despite your actions, despite your words, I LOVE YOU!

I believe unconditional love is what makes the world go round. It's

what creates miracles. Unconditional Love + God.

I wrote this in a notebook and then opened up the book I was reading, A *Return to Love* by Marianne Williamson, and the words looking back at me spoke of love being difficult and that it probably wasn't love if it didn't stretch you in some way.

Isn't that the f*cking truth. Love isn't always easy.

PART TWO

God

chapter 31 | communing with god

There was this knowing that came from the depths of my womanhood. So, while my mind told me it was over and my heart was begging for me to let go, my soul said, *There is something more for you here.* I was called to lean in. I was called to have faith beyond anything that made sense. I was called to release my need to know how this story was going to end.

Nothing about it was logical. My husband was trying to speed up everything to legally secure our separation, while I held on to my soul-knowing that our journey together wasn't over. With every step and with every choice, I was being invited to go deeper. I was invited to pull back another layer. I was invited to return to the truth. I was invited to return to love.

I didn't know what it meant, and I didn't know how, so I asked God to guide me—although at the time I didn't say God. I said Universe, I said Spirit. God knew I meant her and answered every time. The shocking part is that I actually listened. I didn't let my inner rebellious wild child, who thought she always knew best, take over.

I listened when it didn't make sense.

I listened when I didn't want to.

I listened when I got hit with tidal wave after tidal wave.

I listened when I wanted to take the easy route and give up.

I listened when my husband got another woman's initials tattooed on his wedding ring finger, when he told me he didn't believe I was pregnant.

I listened when the answer went against what my human mind told me I "should" be choosing.

Every time I wanted to give up, God told me not to. And she made it abundantly clear. God told me to love deeper and confirmed the fact over and over again that our journey wasn't over. Even though I wanted it to be. I so desperately wanted to walk away so many times. I wanted to say, "F*ck You. We don't need you. We don't want you." But I couldn't. I couldn't speak the words that went against the truth of my soul.

So, my only option was to dig a little deeper, to go deeper within—deeper in the awareness of my soul's truth. Learning lessons in compassion, forgiveness, surrender, faith, trust, love. And I learned it was not just okay but it actually required me to be vulnerable. I learned when I was vulnerable and shared my truth, I not only cracked my heart open but also the hearts of the people around me.

THE MORE CONNECTED I AM TO SELF, THE LESS POWER THE OUTSIDE WORLD HAS OVER ME.

chapter 32 | connection to spirit

This is what tuning into my spiritual nature had really afforded me. The more I connected to God, the more peace I felt. The more I remembered who I was, the less I worried about what other people thought of me. The more I experienced being fully human and fully divine, the less self-judgment, the less guilt, the less shame I had.

The more I saw myself as the creator, the less I saw myself as the victim.

And let's be clear: we are never actually not connected. Our separation from God, our separation from self, and our separation from each other is an illusion.

It hasn't always felt easy for me to tune into my spiritual nature. I resisted it for years. Spirit had knocked at my door many, many times. I felt God's essence around me. I felt Spirit knocking at my door, showing up with champagne, cupcakes, and all life's delights. Sometimes, I would invite her in. I would dabble in prayer, I would talk to my angels, I would have conversations about the magic of the universe. But mostly, I slammed the door right in Spirit's face. Especially when things were going really, really good in my life. Especially when I felt like I had it all. Who needed Spirit? My guest table was full, thank you very much.

I can see in hindsight why this connection to source, connection to spirit, essentially connection to God felt so hard for me for so long. I felt I needed an extra chair for God. I thought God lived outside of me and I needed to invite him in. I didn't realize it was about me connecting inward.

Until the moment I did and then everything changed.

All the rules began to evaporate. What rules, you ask? The rules I had made up. The rules I had been taught. The lies I told myself, and the lies I believed in.

Rule #1: There must be someone between you and God, a master who can translate, so to speak.

Rule #2: You must obey God.

Rule #3: Sacrifice is essential.

Rule #4: God has specific wants for you, and they are very different from your wants.

Rule #5: God knows and you don't.

Rule #6: The devil exists. Be afraid.

Rule #7: God has a plan for you. You better be a good girl and follow it.

Rule #8: There are certain things you must do and not do in order to get to heaven.

Then there was also the spiritual measuring stick I had invented, where I judged how "spiritual" I was on any given day.

Did I pray today?
Did I pray the proper way?
Did I journal?

All spiritual beings journal/write to God every day, don't they?

What about meditation? I couldn't sit in meditation for more than two minutes without thoughts running through my head. Clearly, I was doing it all wrong, which led me to believe there was no point.

So, can you see why it was easier for me to slam the door in Spirit's face when she came knocking? There were times I thought I didn't need her, and times I thought I didn't deserve her. Spirit had no chance with me, until she did. Until my Spiritual Smackdown rolled in. Until God no-optioned me. Until I could no longer slam the door in Spirit's face. It felt like my door blew wide open while I was standing naked in the living room. Either I invited her in, or I walked out into the yard naked.

I chose option #1.

Although option #2 may have been easier.

chapter 33 | choosing peace

Choose Peace.
Choose Peace.
Choose Peace.

At this point in the journey, this became my motto . . . my lifeline, really. It allowed me to anchor into the remembrance of who I was and who we all were.

Yes, even him and even her.

Choosing peace felt like a surrender inward: surrendering to the agenda of my soul, surrendering to the journey, surrendering to the timeline. It began my journey of choosing to respond vs. react, choosing not to send the message in rage, choosing not to invest energy in an-eye-for-an-eye retribution.

And I would love to tell you that from here on out, I sat on the throne of the Goddess in deep remembrance of who I was at all times, but that would be a lie. I chose peace in many, many, many hard moments. I chose vengeance in many moments as well, and each time vengeance was my choice, it created more suffering for all of us.

I started to see that it was suffering of my choosing, and I knew it didn't have to be that way.

Suffering isn't a necessary part of the experience. We create suffering in our response to the experience. But how do we stop this? How do we end the loop of suffering, where the belief creates the experience and the experience validates the belief? We have to bring our awareness to the pattern. We have to shift our perception. And then we have to be willing to choose again, to choose something different, to choose anew.

This is where the work lay for me. The moments I wanted so badly to be right, the moments I wanted to choose self-righteousness, the moments I told myself they deserved it, the moments I wanted to become the villain to cause them pain, the moments it would have been easy to play the victim. I decided to put my inner peace first.

Peace over being right.
Peace over self-righteousness.
Peace over punishment.
Peace over what was "fair."

It wasn't easy to choose this at a human level, but it felt different at a soul level. When I was in meditative states, the resistance seemed to be gone. And so, this is where I started. In meditation, I began by choosing my inner peace. This evolved into me meditating and asking God to guide me in the most peaceful outcome for all of us. Then one day, I heard a whisper from within me that said, "Send him peace, from your heart to his. Send him peace, send him love." And I obeyed.

Multiple times each day, I sat in meditation and prayed for peace and love to be sent to Craig through the ethers. And then a few weeks later, I felt the whisper inside me again. This time, it said to send her peace, send her love.

Absolutely f*cking not was my first thought. This woman who stole my husband, who said she would spit on me if she saw me on the street, who saw me as the villain in the story. The last thing I wanted to do was to extend any sort of compassion to her. I didn't think she deserved it, so I resisted this one hard. It felt so uncomfortable in my body, the thought of doing this. I didn't think I could.

But when I closed my eyes and took a few deep breaths, I felt the portal behind my heart open up. Sending her love felt like truth in my being, and so I did. It wasn't forced, and it didn't feel fake. It felt like divine essence was flowing through me, and it felt surprisingly good. It was a release, a moment when everything felt less heavy, less overwhelming, and less complicated.

And then God showed me what I needed to see. I started to see her in me and me in her. The more I was willing to do this, to see her from this lens, the more I softened, the more peace I felt, and the more I understood. I understood that she was never meant to be the villain in this story, just as I was never meant to be the victim. She, like me, was a woman in pain. She, like me, felt unworthy at times. She, like me, was a woman who was disconnected from the frequency of love.

I knew that any way I viewed her, I was also viewing me. Any way I judged her, I was also judging me. Any way I treated her, I was also treating me. It became so clear to me that I could perpetuate the cycle of blame and shame, I could buy into the belief system of victim and villain, or I could truly shift *from Victim to Goddess* and invite her to do the same by way of the ripple.

I had an inclination of belief then that is solidified now.

Belief that when we shift, we also open up the energetic connection for those around us to shift, whether they are consciously aware of it or not.

This means that anything I do for me, I also do for you. Anything you do for you, you also do for me. It's not selfish to put your frequency first, it's selfless.

Serving me serves you and serves God.

chapter 34 | the voice of god

I became willing to hear the voice of God without even realizing it was the voice of God. What is the voice of God? The voice of God is the voice within you. The voice you hear/feel/experience when you sit with yourself, when you sit in silence, when you sit in a state of being, when you turn off the outside noise.

For many years, I wasn't willing to slow down, to sit in silence, to sit with myself. I was so caught up in living with the "you only live once so do everything" mentality that I forgot this is completely untrue.

You don't only live once. I don't only live once.

We are more than this human body.
We are more than this experience.
We are more than this thought.
We are more than we know ourselves to be.

We forget in order to remember. We act "not of self" in order to become of self. Self being soul. And soul being who we truly are.

Know this.

You are a soul, and the mind and body are tools used to serve the agenda of your soul. Therefore, you are not your mind, and you are not your body. Stop giving so much power to your mind. Stop acting as if you are a body first. When your body ceases to exist, which it will, your soul will remain. Your soul lives on, and you will continue to choose to reincarnate, to come back to earth as long as it serves your soul's agenda.

And know this.

At the core, your soul's agenda is always the same.

To be all that you truly are. To express all that you truly are.

To be love.
To be God.
To be life everlasting.

JOURNAL ENTRY

I know now this needed to happen for me as much as it did for you. I'm grateful you were able to walk away, otherwise we both would have continued to live half alive. I mean I was happy, we were happy . . . so I didn't even realize it, but I can see now that there has been a piece of me missing. My spirituality. I have been denying this part of me, and in doing so, I haven't been living my truth. I will forever be changed by this . . . in a good way. In a way I never knew was possible.

chapter 35 | unconditional love

I looked in the mirror and finally started to see a hint of a belly. I wanted my bump to grow so badly. I was six months pregnant and still, to the outside world, no one could tell. As my reflection looked back at me, I traced my finger along the slight curve of my stomach and then across the tattoo that runs along the side of my body. I often forget it's there, the tattoos Craig and I got on our honeymoon.

Mine reads "Family . . . where life begins and love never ends." When I got these words permanently inked on my skin, I had no idea of the experience that was coming and how deeply I would be called to hold the frequency of this love.

Could I stay true to those words in that moment? In the moment that I was creating a new life, I could feel the strong presence of my baby girl growing inside me—this is where life begins. But what about the love never ending part? What about my love for Craig? Did it have to end? I grabbed a marker, and I wrote on the bathroom mirror:

I have faith in our journey, I have faith in our love, I have faith our

journeys are leading back together.

I ran out of room on the bathroom mirror, so I ran and grabbed my journal. I continued to scribble down these words . . .

I have faith that this isn't the end of the road for us, but either way, I

know I will continue to carry you in my heart and continue to learn

from the lessons our relationship and this heartache is teaching me.

In that moment, love seemed so clear to me. I had never felt the power of love like that before. I continued to write:

Unconditionally loving you means loving you whether or not you love me in return. Unconditionally loving you means seeing the light in you even when you don't see it in yourself.

I love you more than I knew. I love you more deeply than I ever thought I could love someone. I have it in me to forgive more than I ever thought possible. I am less angry than I thought I would be.

The next time I heard from Craig, he told me he was about to leave on a two-and-a-half-week vacation to Portugal. My initial reaction was to compete and compare. I thought about the fact that we hadn't traveled together in a long time. Craig had been saying for the last year it was too hard for him to take the time off while his company was so new. I felt I had every reason and every right to be mad. But I knew that it ultimately wasn't going to serve me and so I chose peace.

I asked myself what I could do that would result in the outcome I so desperately wanted, the outcome of peace. And not just for me, but for him and for us. And the answer was to not put up a fight, to not complain about the time he was missing with Kane, and to use that time to go deeper on my journey with myself.

The day he left, I decided to write him a real letter, one that I vowed to give him when he returned home from Portugal. I told him all I wanted was for there to be peace between us. I wanted the conflict to die. I wanted to do whatever was going to make him happy so that he could fully show up for his kids. I told him I would stop being the cause of him needing to live two separate lives, and that I was willing to allow Kane and Hannah to meet so he could stop needing to choose between him and her.

chapter 36 | love

It sounds simple, doesn't it . . .

> . . . return to love.
> . . . love is a choice.
> . . . love heals.

I promise you, it's not. It's not simple. But you are not here for simple.

You are here for your soul's expansion. You are here to experience being the creator and to understand that with each decision, you shift the universe. You are here to embody the truth of your soul. You are here to literally be love.

chapter 37 | forgiveness

I had continued sending Craig and Hannah peace and love in my meditations. While it felt good, I knew there was more to it. For me to be able to follow through on the vow to myself, for me to actually be able to hand that letter over to him, I needed to let go of my anger, and I needed to find a way to forgive him.

I knew it was necessary—but I didn't feel like I knew what forgiveness even meant. I had never really understood forgiveness, it felt so superficial to me.

Someone says they're sorry, the other person accepts the apology, says it's okay, and then everyone moves on. But oftentimes we say this, we say it's okay, we move on, but we bank the memory and save it to pull out the next time we have a grievance with that person. I'm a pro at this. I have held on to grudges since I was a child. Forgiveness never really felt like forgiveness, that saying "forgive but don't forget"; well, to me, there is nothing forgiving about it.

I knew I couldn't just say the words this time; I had to do the work. I had to turn inward and excavate all that was ready to be excavated. I felt willing to do this, but I had no idea how, so I went back to writing. I sat with a blank page before me and asked God for guidance in helping me to forgive Craig.

I sat in the silence and in stillness for a few minutes and then I reached my hand out for a red pen, not the typical black I usually write with. I remembered Craig's previous words to me, when he said he "started seeing red." Red represented his anger, so I let the red represent mine as well.

I wrote page after page in red pen. Pages of questioning, pages of rage, pages of how could you, pages of f*ck you, letting all the anger pour out of me. It felt good. It felt good to not hold any of it in, to feel wildly unleashed.

The pages began with the anger and the f*ck-you energy toward Craig and then I turned my anger and f*ck-you energy to God. How could he let this happen, how could he continue to let this happen, how come he didn't protect my babies? Oh, I had questions and anger piled up for God.

And then all of a sudden, the red pen turned on me. I had anger, rage, f*ck-you energy, and judgments toward myself. I wrote about the moments I had betrayed myself, the moments I had dishonored myself, the moments I had ignored my intuition. So much stored inside.

It was clear to see that Craig was not the person I was being led to forgive, not yet anyway. Before I could forgive Craig, I needed to forgive God. And before I could forgive God, I needed to forgive myself.

FORGIVING ME

For as long as I can remember, I've been desperately searching for love. Although if you watch my life like a movie, you may not see it. You'd see the outside:

The wild child.
The party girl.
The fierce boss.
The girl who told her friends she wanted to be a single mom so no one else could influence how her kids were raised.

It was all a front. Inside, I yearned to be loved, but I also said I didn't believe in love, which created a massive conflict within my being. How does one experience love when she's not open to love?

I saw two pathways. One where I could be soft, open, vulnerable, and available, which left me wide open to be hurt and heartbroken. Or I could be rigid, protective, and fiercely guarding of my heart to avoid pain at all costs.

I chose the latter, but there was something I was wrong about. The pain could not be avoided, because it's not meant to be. And in the ruse of choosing pleasure to avoid the pain, I experienced more pain. Pain that was unbearable at times because over and over and over again, I felt the pain of self-betrayal, and I discovered that the wounds of self-betrayal are the wounds that cut the deepest.

I see them so clearly now, each self-inflicted cut leaving its mark. Each time I dishonored myself, each time I dishonored others, each time I didn't speak my truth, each time I ignored my intuition, each time I closed off my heart, each time I said words I didn't mean, each time I pushed someone away, each time I took actions that didn't represent the truth of who I am or what I felt, each time I chose fear over love.

Fear disguised as independence.
Fear disguised as strength.
Fear disguised as power.

My forgiveness of self needed to begin here. I needed to forgive myself for the lies I told myself and then believed. I needed to forgive myself for the pain I caused others. I needed to forgive myself for the love I experienced and threw away in my twenties. I needed to forgive myself for the teenage girl who denied herself from the very beginning.

I could sit here and say I didn't know better. I was so young; gosh, I was only fifteen. Or I can see through the eyes of truth. I did know because we always know. I knew I was betraying myself. There are moments I remember so vividly; the warning signs, the intuition, the red flags I completely ignored. It would be easy to say I didn't know, but that would be a lie. I knew, as we always do.

I knew I was choosing an unhealthy pathway, but I didn't have the awareness to know that I knew. I didn't have the awareness to know that the pathway I was choosing was one that would lead me deeper into the illusion and one that would move me further from love.

I began here, writing about the experience when I was fifteen years old, and then the words "and I forgive myself."

And then I moved on to Mike, Kurt, Ben, Ryan . . . and finally Spencer. The one I ran from, the one who almost cracked me open. There were many layers of self-judgment I was holding on to with him.

I had to forgive myself for not allowing my heart to be safe with him, because the truth is, it was. My heart was safe with him, but his heart wasn't safe with me. I wasn't available to allow my heart to crack open, and the closer he got, the harder and further I pushed away. It was too risky to choose anything else because that would require me to go somewhere I wasn't yet willing to go. I wasn't willing to meet myself in truth.

There was a lot to process in these past relationships where I rejected love. With everything laid out before me, I could see the sabotage so clearly. I could see the girl who was so scared to be let down, the girl who feared being rejected, who feared not being loved, who feared not being enough. So, she entered relationships, knowing that they were destructive.

I went through twenty years of memories, from the age of fifteen to thirty-five, and with each memory, each experience that came pouring forth, I would write one or two sentences and the words "and I forgive myself." One or two sentences again "and I forgive myself." And on it went. I wrote the words "and I forgive myself" at least one hundred times over, one after the other.

And this brought me to Craig. There were things that had transpired within my marriage that also required forgiveness of self.

This is what I wrote:

I wish I told you how deeply I truly love you, instead of telling you I love Kane more than you, which was never really true. And I FORGIVE MYSELF.

I wish I told you how much I appreciate everything you do for us, the sacrifices you make for us and how hard you work for us. I am not sure why I expressed this to everyone but you. And I FORGIVE MYSELF.

I wish we talked about losing our last baby. I wish I asked you how you were dealing with it. I wish I told you how much my heart hurt. I wish I didn't shut you out. And I FORGIVE MYSELF.

I wish I came to your opening night at work, to support you and show you how proud I am of you. And I FORGIVE MYSELF.

I wish I told you every day that I think you are the most amazing dad. I still feel this way. I am so thankful this is a bond we will share forever, and I am so grateful my kids get to live life with you as their dad. And I FORGIVE MYSELF.

I wish I had focused on us more. I wish we had gone out, drank wine, laughed, talked, connected, just the two of us as a couple, not as parents. And I FORGIVE MYSELF.

I wish I didn't give so much to my business. I wish I put my phone down. I wish I put my computer down. I wish I was more present. And I FORGIVE MYSELF.

I wish I got up to start our day together. I wish I crawled into bed at the same time as you so we could end our day together. And I FORGIVE MYSELF.

I wish I didn't say no the last time you wanted to have sex. I don't know why I was so scared those first few months of this pregnancy. I wish I told you how I was feeling instead of just pushing you away. And I FORGIVE MYSELF.

I wish I was a better wife. I love Kane like crazy and love being his mama, but I wish I didn't let the role of being his mom consume me. I have the capacity to be a great mom and a great wife at the same time. I wish I took care of you too. And I FORGIVE MYSELF.

Mostly, I wish I didn't stop being me. I wish I didn't lose myself. I wish I continued to be the fun-loving Jak you fell in love with. The woman you married. And I FORGIVE MYSELF.

Where to begin. After writing the letter to him and after forgiving myself, I felt like so much had been cleared away. I understood that we each had a whole lifetime of experiences, stories, memories, traumas stacked up against us, influencing the choices we were making today.

I saw where fear was mostly leading.
I saw where judgment was in control.

And I realized to truly forgive Craig, I needed to stop judging him.

I needed to stop judging him, and I needed to stop feeling sorry for myself. I needed to stop shaming him; I needed to stop wanting him to feel guilty. I began to see that my judgment of him and that my lack of forgiveness were contributing to him remaining in the state he was in. It wasn't going to help him move forward, it was perpetuating the cycle, keeping him stuck in the role he was fulfilling. The guilt and shame I'd been placing on him fostered fear, not growth. It fostered control, not acceptance.

I understood this conceptually, but how was I going to shift from judgment to forgiveness? Via compassion, that's how. I was able to start forgiving myself when I had compassion for myself, when I released judgment about my past actions, when I told myself I was doing what I thought was best in that moment. This allowed me to look at myself through the eyes of love, to see the beauty in all of the messiness, in all of the "mistakes." Now I was being invited to do the same for Craig. I was being invited into the frequency of acceptance, to accept where he was at in his journey so I could see the divine essence in him, and so I could mirror it back.

Of course, this seemed to roll in and out with the tide. I felt forgiveness in my heart, but my mind often tried to take me back to a place of anger, a place of hurt, a place of betrayal. When my mind tried to jeopardize this, when I slipped into judgment, I asked the universe for help. I asked the universe to show me.

And what she showed me, what I witnessed, was that Craig was now running from love, just as I once did. He was self-sabotaging, chasing pleasure in an attempt to avoid pain.

His actions told the story: the spending spree he had been on, the trips, the sex, the drugs, the alcohol. He was desperately chasing something he thought was love, I could understand this. I thought I was too. If he was anything like me, he was really chasing the feeling of worthiness; he wanted to feel worthy of love.

FORGIVING HER

A few days went by and I felt like I had truly forgiven myself and Craig, but there was something still feeling off, something that was lingering, and it felt like it was just beyond my awareness.

I went back to my journal to see all that I had processed the past few days.

I had raged at and forgiven Craig.

I had unleashed on and forgiven God.

I had gone deeply inward and forgiven myself.

But there was still the question I left, the one I wrote in big bold letters that said: Who am I attacking or not forgiving?

The answer was so obviously clear. Hannah. But how could I even begin to forgive this woman? Sending her peace was one thing, but forgiveness was a whole other thing. We're talking about the woman who poisoned my husband against me, the woman who said I was manipulating him with my daughter's health, the woman who said I was pretending to be pregnant as a trap.

How could God tell me that this woman deserved my forgiveness? She was the cause of all my pain. She was the reason my husband and son were separated. She was the reason why my daughter was being abandoned before she was even born. She knew exactly what she was getting involved in, and she chose it.

It took me a while to reconcile this within myself, to come to terms with my desire to forgive her, and then it became really quite simple. I realized that my forgiveness was not just for her, it was also for me. She likely didn't care if I forgave her or not. I needed to forgive her for my own well-being, so I could return to love and so I could reclaim my inner peace.

To forgive her, I needed to shift the way I viewed her. I couldn't keep calling her a homewrecker and his mistress. I had to start seeing her beyond what I knew her to be, beyond this experience.

So, I started to explore the possibility that Hannah was put in Craig's path for a reason, and maybe even in my path for a reason. What if she came into our life to help us learn lessons we had both failed to learn before? What if there was a lesson for her to learn on her journey through him? And what if once these lessons were learned, they would part ways?

I started to see how forgiving her allowed me to further forgive myself. I looked back at all I had written in the previous days, remembering I was lost at once too. I looked at the relationship I had engaged in when I was scared of being hurt, scared of being betrayed, and scared of being let down. This is when I entered relationships that I knew deep down were destructive. I feared love. I closed my heart to love.

And I remembered that when my heart was closed to love, when I was living in fear, when I felt unworthy, I also hurt others.

In a way, probably in many ways, she and I were more similar than I wanted to admit. I started to relate to her. I saw bits of myself and bits of my past relationships in her. I saw in her the parts in myself from my past that I had not forgiven myself for. I had walked in her shoes before; I put out fear-based, unloving energy into the world. "Do unto others as you would have do unto you" was not something I lived by. I had disrespected love.

As I began to see the innocence in her, I reminded myself that I did not know her journey. I did not know what had brought her to that point. I did not know her past. I did not know what lay ahead in her future. What I did know was it was none of my business. That was between her and God. Because she, too, is a child of God.

And I thought she most certainly felt some of the same fears I felt in previous relationships: fear that he wouldn't choose her, fear that he wasn't there for good, fear that he would go back to his family, which all represented the underlying fear I once had too. The fear that I was not worthy of love, that I didn't deserve love.

This is likely why she put up such a fight whenever he and I were meant to have any engagement together: the time I had asked him to meet us at the park, the mediation sessions with Lisa, the day we biked to his work. She feared he would choose us.

I knew there would likely be many moments to come when I would waver in how I chose to view her. So, to remind myself, I wrote down a list of actions I could take/not take:

I decided I would not judge her or talk badly about her with others. I would avoid looking at her Instagram. I would continue to send her loving energy and peaceful thoughts. I would choose not to react to external circumstances. I would stop thinking attack thoughts, and if attack thoughts entered, I'd ask God to step in and replace them with thoughts of peace. I'd pray to see things from a different perspective. And I decided that I would remember.

I would remember she is a child of God.
She is on her own spiritual journey.
She has lost her way
And it was not my job to monitor her spiritual path.

This I clearly knew was true and I wrote it down so I wouldn't forget:

I am not here to judge Craig's or Hannah's spiritual progress. When I stop judging them and start accepting them as they are, miracles are possible. By remaining awake to their beauty, I can subconsciously remind them of who they are.

This time, my prayer to God was simple:

I am willing to see this situation; I am willing to see him and willing to see her through another lens. I invite the Holy Spirit in to maneuver and work miracles. Amen.

And I reminded myself why all of this forgiveness was so important, because the truth is, I knew forgiveness would give us all freedom.

THE PATHWAY
TO TRUE FORGIVENESS
OPENED UP WHEN
*I REALIZED
THERE WAS
NOTHING
TO FORGIVE.*

chapter 38 | judgment

I stopped judging them. I stopped seeing their actions as "wrong." And I began to see they were both just searching for love, but they were controlled by fear. Fear of not being loved, fear of not being enough, fear of being abandoned.

When I stopped judging them for what they had done, and when I stopped judging the act of infidelity itself, the need for forgiveness evaporated. If there was nothing wrong, if there was nothing bad, how could there be something to forgive?

There simply was what was in that moment, as there is what is in this moment.

I started to see forgiveness as an illusion. It doesn't truly exist; forgiveness is never truly needed. All that is required is to release the judgment.

When judgment of self ceases to exist.
When judgment of others ceases to exist.
Forgiveness ceases to exist.

We return to our God-like state.

Without fully understanding it at the time, I was seeing through the eyes of God. I was seeing him for who he is. Her for who she is. Me for who I am.

And it went against everything I had always thought.

I was the woman who said, "I would never."
I would never stay with a man who betrayed me.

I wouldn't be like them, all the women I had witnessed turn a blind eye, the women who accepted it and still proclaimed to love the cheaters.

I was strong. Independent. I didn't need a man. I didn't need love . . . or so I thought.

God no-optioned me into seeing otherwise.
God no-optioned me into experiencing the full capacity of my heart.

He showed me where my limitations existed. And not at the human level, at the soul level. He invited me to see beyond what I could see with my human eyes that were tainted by my human pains.

I started to see the oneness within us.

I started to see them as me and me as them.
I started to see we weren't so different, he, she, and me.

I recognized I thought I knew what I would have chosen in their shoes, but truly I didn't.
None of us ever does.

chapter 39 | the villains

Suffering is an illusion.
Victimhood is an illusion.

So, if suffering is an illusion
and victimhood is an illusion

Where does this leave the villains . . .
Spoiler alert: there are none.

Villainhood is an illusion.

Another hard pill to swallow: If there are no villains, does that mean there is no right and wrong? No good and bad? At a soul level, yes, this is true. If you look through the eyes of God, you will see that.

But what about looking through your human eyes? This is where a shift in perspective is required. Instead of seeing yourself as the judge, the jury, the prosecutor . . . can you zoom out? Can you remove yourself from these roles? And choose what brings you the most inner peace?

This requires the letting go of many things:

The need to be right.
The want to be vindicated.
The desire to see those who have "wronged" you, or others, get what's coming to them.

It means releasing self-righteousness.
It means choosing love over pain.
It means choosing your love for you, above all else.

So, we need to learn to love ourselves first.

To love ourselves from within.

To not make our love of self dependent on anything or anyone outside of us.

What happens if you look at every experience in your life—the current experiences, the past experiences, the future experiences—as opportunities to rise *from Victim to Goddess*. To harness your personal power. To deepen your self-awareness. To choose your peace above all else.

KARMA
IS NOT
A BITCH.

chapter 40 | putting down the sword

I was still sending Craig and Hannah peace and love daily while they were away. Strangely, it started to feel like the three of us were moving through an experience, not the two of them and me separately. Of course, they didn't feel this, not consciously at least, but I could feel massive shifts being created for all of us, and I felt it amplify since I became willing to include her in my prayers and meditations.

I think that's why it felt like such a shock to my system when he came back from his trip and was intensely angry at me. I had moved through such deep layers of forgiveness; I had sent all the love through the ethers. I felt peace and was ready to hand over the letter telling him peace was all I wanted and I was willing to give in. But he returned mad, and he was mad because I had the expectation that when he got home, we'd go back to our regular schedule. He would see Kane that Tuesday and Thursday, plus have a weekend sleepover like they typically did at his mom's.

This was the piece that was still left for me; I needed to release my expectations. And while my expectation might seem fair, it truly wasn't, because again I knew something he didn't know I knew. I knew there was another event coming up. I saw the planned birthday celebration because I was still checking his email.

Her thirtieth birthday fell on the same day he was supposed to be with Kane, the first night he was scheduled to see our son after not seeing him for three weeks. I saw the email, but I held out hope he would choose Kane, which I had somehow construed into believing meant he was choosing us over her.

Either way, he didn't make the choice I wanted him to make. He chose her, of course, asking me to switch days for his time with Kane.

My instinct was to rage, to guilt him, to shame him, to try to make him feel like a horrible human for even asking, for not racing to see his child the moment his plane landed. I wanted to lash out; I wanted to make up an excuse for why that was a no; I wanted to say if you don't want him Tuesday, then you can't have him Wednesday.

But then, I simply decided to stop.

I decided to put down the attack sword. I decided to stop trying to control things, to stop trying to set him up for failure, to stop trying to show him how wrong his decisions were, to stop trying to make him even choose.

I decided to stop playing the game, which allowed me to invite in peace. It was collectively felt.

The next day, Craig and I ran into each other on the street. My belly had finally popped while he was away, so this was the first time he saw me actually looking like I was pregnant. I saw it instantly in his eyes: the truth that our baby girl was coming registered in that moment.

He instinctively reached out his hand to touch my belly but pulled back before he did, realizing what he was about to do. He was about to touch me; he wanted to touch me. It felt right and wrong in the very same moment. He pulled back his hand, hoping he would no longer feel the urge to reach for me, but he still felt it, so he asked for permission.

When I said yes, he touched my belly for the first time in months, feeling her essence. As he felt her, I felt him, and I let my guard down. I decided to let him see the vulnerable side of me he had so rarely seen, even throughout our relationship. I didn't intend to, but the moment I started to speak, the tears started to softly flow.

I told him how confused I still was and also how much I wanted to find a way to be at peace with each other. I told him I wanted us to remember the love that created these two humans so that we could find a way to parent them in a loving environment, and I told him I was willing to do whatever it took to create that.

His reaction surprised me. Letting my wall down appeared to give him permission to let his wall down too. The softness he saw in me opened the softness in him. And there, on the side of the street that we had been in a car chase on two months earlier, he put his hand back on my belly and said, "We're going to figure this out."

I had no idea what he meant, he had no idea what he meant, but his words felt true.

As he walked away, the tears fully streamed down my face. I knew this already; I knew in my heart we were going to be okay, that we'd figure this out. I knew we were going to be led back together and sometimes it felt like that made it harder. I wanted to skip to that part where it was all figured out. I didn't want to continue to experience the pain that was also part of this experience. The pain of being left behind while my husband walked away to go celebrate his girlfriend's birthday.

I let the tears of knowing mixed with tears of sadness flow, hanging onto the fact that I had felt a massive shift between us and I could tell he'd felt it too.

I was right. I received a text from him later that day. The message itself wasn't huge. He simply said thanks for changing days with him and he was excited to see Kane tomorrow. It was the fact that he had sent a text that was huge. It meant, after our exchange that morning, he had finally unblocked me from his phone.

This is the thing I had been praying for. I wanted to know I had a way to get through to Craig when I needed to, that if something happened with Kane or if I went into labor, I'd be able to contact the father of my children.

JOURNAL ENTRY

There is a piece of me that actually thinks it took courage to do what you did. I gave you all the opportunity in the world to stay, to put a Band-Aid solution on, to just pretend you didn't have an affair, to just pretend we were happy. I can't imagine where we'd be at right now had you just stayed. I don't think in a good place. I would be holding onto so much resentment.

It took me a while to get here, but I am starting to feel grateful you said no. I often think about the tattoo on your leg: "Live, live fully, without regrets." I admire you for living your life this way, even amidst all the backlash and judgment you received from me, your family, your friends. It wasn't fair for any of us to react that way. I am sorry for the role I played in this. This experience has taught me more than you will ever know. I feel like a completely different woman in the best way.

LYING
IS POISON
TO YOUR BODY
AND IT'S
POISON TO
YOUR SOUL.

chapter 41 | poison

When you don't tell the truth, it's poison to your body and it's poison to your soul. And guess who you lie to the most often?

YOU.

You're so willing to lie to yourself.
To tell yourself untruths and then believe them.

Every time you question yourself.
Every time you doubt.
Every time you worry.
Every time you let fear win.

You lie to yourself about who you truly are.

You are a creator.
You are a being of infinite, limitless potential.

Start acting like it.
Stop believing the lies you tell yourself.
Start living the truth of your soul.

You came here for a reason.
Remember that.

And don't let anyone else ever tell you anything different.

WHEN I ASKED YOU WHAT
YOU TRULY WANTED
AND YOU WERE BRAVE ENOUGH
TO ANSWER,
IN COMPLETE HONESTY,
IT OPENED UP A PORTAL,
A GATEWAY FOR THE
*MIRACLES TO
ENTER.*

chapter 42 | choosing again

The day came when it was time for me to give him the letter I wrote. I was prepared to tell my husband I wasn't going to stand in his way any longer. I wasn't going to make him choose between her and our kids. He could have both.

I returned to our house on one of the nights Craig was with Kane. Part of me was hoping he had time to talk, and part of me was hoping that he didn't. He was upstairs putting Kane to bed when I walked in the door, so I sat on the couch, waiting and thinking about the letter. Once I handed it over, there would be no turning back. I was willing to do whatever it took to create real peace and harmony between us, and allowing Hannah to meet Kane seemed to be the solution.

When Craig came downstairs, he sat on the couch beside me. This was not normal; he usually raced to get out of the house the moment I walked in the door. I decided if he was going to sit beside me, I was going to take the opportunity to talk to him before I handed over the goods.

I turned to him and asked if he was happy. He said no, which wasn't that surprising since he was living a life where he was not with Kane every day. I told him that I wanted my kids to have a happy dad and said I wanted to work together to get him to a happy place.

Then I asked, "In your ideal world, what would make you happy?"

I fully expected him to say he wanted the white-picket-fence fairy-tale life with Hannah. He wanted her, and he wanted our kids there with them half the time. I held my breath as I waited for this answer, already knowing I was going to say yes, because I truly wanted peace and I was willing to do whatever it took. Yes was going to be my answer to whatever he asked for, to whatever was going to make him happy.

I was prepared to give that yes, but the answer I thought I was going to get was not the answer I got. He told me in his ideal world, he would sleep on the couch in our house so he could fall asleep with Kane every day and wake up with him every morning.

My heart broke when I heard this, and even more so when I told him we both knew that wasn't realistic and it also wasn't what he really wanted. And then I asked him the exact same question again. He looked me in the eye and repeated what he had just said; he would sleep on the couch every night so he could be with his son every day.

At this point, I tried to feed him his answer. I asked him if he wanted the white-picket-fence house and life with Hannah and his kids. He said he thought he did, but he wasn't sure anymore. I knew at that moment, he would never see my letter. If he wasn't sure he even wanted it, I wasn't about to give it.

And then he turned the tables and started questioning me. He asked me why I was still wearing my wedding ring, something many people had been asking me for many months. I wanted to say I am still wearing my wedding ring because I believe we are going to find our way back to each other, because it is a symbol of our love that I know is still there, because I vowed to never take it off.

But that is not what I said. I froze, feeling the words get caught in my throat. I heard the lies as I was speaking them, but I didn't stop myself; I didn't admit to him that I was telling him a bunch of lies. I just let the lies come out.

I told him that the ring obviously didn't mean anything anymore, but because I love it and because it's a gorgeous piece of jewelry, I was going to keep wearing it while I still could, while we were still technically married.

As these words left my mouth, the wall between us went back up, the conversation ended, and Craig got up and walked out the door.

I instantly regretted saying those words, telling Craig the ring on my finger meant nothing. And when I woke up the next morning, I made a choice. I decided that I was free to choose again. I decided that just because I acted out of alignment, I didn't need to continue to let that energy live between him and me, so I sent him a text.

"I didn't tell you the truth last night. You live with another woman, and that makes it hard for me to say these words to you. I don't think our story is over, and I don't want our story to be over. I love you. That's why I am still wearing my wedding ring."

There it was, my original words retracted and my truth sent out.

I had anticipated fear to come creeping in, the fear of rejection telling me that would never happen. But it didn't. What I felt was relief. It was a relief to tell him that despite the fact we were going back and forth with divorce lawyers, I still believed in us.

And from there, the floodgates opened.

Craig responded with a flood of texts, but it was the last one I responded to.

C: When Kane tells me he wants Dadda and Mama, it rips my heart out.

Me: He told me the other day, "Dadda loves Mama the most . . . that one tore through my heart."

C: He's right, though, I hope you know that.

Um, what? No, I did not know that. In fact, everything that had happened in the past few months led me to believe the exact opposite of that. But the day Kane had said this to me, I did wonder for a fraction of a second if he knew something I didn't. He, like all kids, was so intuitive. And almost every time I had asked God to give me a sign that it was time for me to throw in the towel on my marriage, it would be Kane who would give me one of the signs. It's how I knew it was worth continuing to hold on.

I asked Craig where he thought we took such a wrong turn. And I also asked him a hard question that I wasn't sure I actually wanted him to answer: I asked him if he fell out of love with me or just fell more in love with her.

"Neither," he said. "We've been through a lot that no one understands, and our communication skills suck. You started to get angry, and I started to see red too, and then I started making bad decisions. She was just a good out. I didn't really think about you or Kane, I just thought it was easier to leave, and now I kill myself for it."

I asked him what he thought would happen if we just decided to run away and live on a beach together like we used to dream about. He said he thought it would be amazing and that he'd love to leave this all behind and press the reset button.

But he also said he didn't know how I'd ever forgive him.

He didn't realize I already had.

We ended the conversation by both admitting to each other that we didn't want this to be the end of us, and we decided he would come pick us up at the beach the next weekend so we could have a real talk, face-to-face, to figure out if our marriage was worth another shot.

The week felt wobbly. Throughout the day, we would talk a lot and then at night when he was with her, he would go dark. The message God was sending me was received loud and clear. Continue to choose peace, surrender that which you don't know, and have faith.

We had planned for him to come pick us up on Saturday. In hindsight, I realized this was a day he could get away with telling her he had to work and she would never know. But then, mid-week, my gramma passed away, and her funeral was being held on the Sunday, which put a big question mark on everything.

We were four months into our separation, and I still hadn't told my dad. It was the conversation I had been dreading the most. I literally thought it would kill him to not only know I was hurting, but Craig was also like the son he never had. When I told Craig I was finally going to have to tell my dad because I couldn't think of another excuse for why my husband wouldn't be attending my gramma's funeral, he said, "Don't."

"Don't tell your dad. I will be there and then you, Kane, and I can come home and we can chat. Maybe your dad will never need to know."

Tears streamed down my face when I heard him say that. I knew he felt what I felt. And maybe he didn't know it yet, not in his mind, but in his soul he felt what I had always felt. The truth that our story wasn't over.

There was no maybe about it. If Craig showed up to my gramma's funeral, I knew I would never tell my dad.

This was Thursday, and then for the next seventy-two hours, I didn't hear a word from him. I kept feeling pulled to reach out to him, I kept jumping to the conclusion that he wasn't going to show up, I kept doubting, but I also kept choosing to see the way my mind was playing tricks on me, and I kept coming back to trust. And I asked God to resolve this for me.

Sunday morning I got a text: "I'm still coming, but I might be late." I responded right away but the message went undelivered, and up until two minutes before the funeral started, I was still holding out hope, trusting in his word although almost every promise he had made to me in the past few months had been broken. And that's when he walked through the door, took a seat beside me, and pulled Kane onto his lap.

After the funeral, we embarked on a two-hour drive back to the city together. Almost immediately, Kane fell asleep, giving us plenty of time to talk. Craig and I had done this drive a million times before, and we had had some of our best conversations on this road.

Craig initiated the conversation, saying ever since we had that conversation on the couch, he had been wondering if there was a way back for us. I told him there would always be a way back; we had the luxury of choosing and choosing again. Nothing was permanent unless we chose it to be.

He broke down. He revealed events from his childhood, ones he had previously said he didn't remember. They all revolved around him being left, and many revolved around his father not showing up for him.

He told me about a time he sat waiting on his front steps for hours because his dad promised he was coming, and how those two hours turned into two years before he saw him again. He told me that Hannah was filling a void, and he knew it. She was a pretty mask that made it easier to hide everything he was feeling. He said he wanted his family back and his life back, but he also didn't think he deserved us, me, or his children. He said he wanted to believe we could come out of this together, but he just didn't see how it was possible.

How could we ever go back? He knew things would never be the same again and that scared him. But that was the point. We weren't supposed to go back; I didn't want to go back to where we had come from. I had grown. I felt different, I felt better, I felt good. And to be honest, other than the heartbreak I felt between him and me, I had never felt better in my life.

I was solid in my beliefs and thankful for my connection to God. I was being guided by spirit. I felt the strong presence of our baby girl inside of me. I had passed the twenty-eight-week mark when the doctors thought they might have to induce, and I knew she was going to hang on.

I deeply believed in the words "this or something better," and I believed this about our marriage. I believed the something better was waiting for us, and I was happy that things would never be the same again.

He wanted to believe me; he wanted to trust in my words. He told me how scared he was about giving us another chance and it not working. He was scared I would never be able to forgive him, and he was scared that I would hold it against him forever and punish him for the rest of our lives. He was scared that I would seek an eye-for-an-eye retribution, that it would be the first thing to come up in arguments. And he said he was scared because he knew he wouldn't be able to handle it the way I had if the roles were ever reversed.

This is where his fear voice lived. One of the things he'd always been afraid of was me leaving him. It's what he knew: those who love him, leave him. This reaffirmed what he had told my mom right after we separated when she asked him what had happened. He had said to her, "Jaclyn doesn't need me. She has Kane and her business and now this new baby. She doesn't need me."

And he was right. At the time, I didn't think I needed him . . . but I wanted him and I let him know that. I asked him if he preferred to be needed or wanted. Because Hannah was making it very clear that she needed him. She needed him and we wanted him. I told him he had a choice to make. Going where he was needed felt safer and going where he was wanted was scary, because wants can change, needs don't.

As we got close to the city, he asked how I could ever really forgive him. How I could forgive him for all the pain he caused me and for putting our daughter's life in jeopardy. He thought the stress I felt is what caused my pregnancy complications, and he struggled to believe that this was not the case. He wanted to punish himself.

This is when I told him I didn't need to forgive him because I already had. And not on a surface-level aspect of forgiveness, not like the Band-Aid solution I tried to apply at the beginning. It wasn't in the frequency of "forgive and forget" either. Because it wasn't about forgetting, it was about accepting, understanding, and viewing both him and myself through the eyes of God, the eyes of love.

I told him I had forgiven him, I had forgiven her, and I had forgiven myself. This last part confused him. Why did I need to forgive myself? And so, I told him about all the ways I had betrayed myself when it came to love.

I told him about the walls that had been in place. And I told him about my desire to run.

Then I told him the truth about what I felt about forgiveness. I told him that my forgiveness wasn't dependent on him and what he chose or didn't choose. My forgiveness didn't require him to say, "I'm sorry." Forgiveness for me was about dropping the judgment.

WHEN TRUTH
MEETS TRUTH,
THE MIRACLE
SEES HER
PATHWAY.

chapter 43 | miracle frequency

The distortions are revealed. The limitations, creating obstacles in the miracle pathway, are removed. Because truth is the most powerful frequency there is. Truth is the frequency of knowing, truth is the frequency of creation, truth is the frequency of faith, truth is the frequency of love. And the most important truth you will ever express is the truth of who you are. The truth that comes from your soul, not your mind.

I know because I know.

I am because I am.

These are two incredibly powerful statements. These statements represent you standing in conviction of who you are, without waver, without validation, without needing anything outside of yourself in order for you to be who you are. This is the frequency you're meant to move from, do from, create from. Not from the knowing in your mind but the knowing in your soul.

Now here's the thing about this soul-knowing, though; you may not understand it, in the beginning, when your truth appears. It feels illogical.

"I know because I know because I know," but the knowing is hard to grasp. It makes no sense and makes perfect sense at the same time. It feels like it makes no sense because at the level of the human mind it doesn't, not in human terms. You can't prove what you know. You don't have any evidence of it being real or true, but it's also an undeniable knowing that you have. It makes so much sense at a soul level.

And here's the thing I came to realize: Your mind doesn't need to get it. It doesn't need to get any of it. You don't need to get your mind on board. Your soul sees and knows things that your human mind can't comprehend. So, allow it, don't interfere, don't get in the way. Let "I know because I know because I know" be all the evidence that you need to deepen in trust and move from a place of faith.

IT'S EITHER
NOT YET OR
SOMETHING
*BETTER IS
EN ROUTE.*

chapter 44 | conviction

What's the fastest way to step into alignment?

Stay true to who you are.
Stand unwaveringly in conviction.

Notice where you're tempted to step outside yourself.
Where you drop your personal power.
Where you compare . . . compete . . . judge.

You are on a soul journey that is unique to you.
She is on a soul journey that is unique to her.
He is on a soul journey that is unique to him.

Don't let "who you are" and "who they are" create distortions in your energy field. Don't let "your timeline" and "their timeline" distract you.

All is happening for you in service of your soul's agenda.

It's either not YET or something better is en route.
This is the frequency to hold.

chapter 45 | moving forward

As we returned home after the funeral, Craig ended the conversation by telling me he was ready to talk to someone, and he'd made an appointment to see a therapist he had seen in the past. He held my hand as he said, "I'm going to make changes in my life so there is no one else in it. Let's see if we can get back on track."

The relief I felt was palpable. Without her in the picture, it felt like we'd at least have a chance to see if our marriage was salvageable.

We decided he'd move into our rental condo that had recently been vacated, and we'd take it from there. Even though that meant that night he was still going home to her, I believed him. Him being with her no longer meant he didn't love me.

A couple nights later when he was having one of his nights with Kane, I came home to the two of them cuddled in my bed. I climbed in and we hung out, the three of us, until Kane fell asleep. As Kane's eyes closed, Craig got up, walked over to my side of the bed, knelt down, kissed my belly and asked if he could stay. I said no, I wasn't willing to go there, not while he was still living with someone else.

I had decided I wouldn't give him an ultimatum; that's not how I wanted our journey finding our way back together to begin. But I also didn't want it to start with me feeling like the other woman. Was that the right choice, I truly don't know. Craig was looking for certainty; he wanted to feel needed. His fears kept coming forward. He couldn't fully trust in my forgiveness, it was hard for him to believe that I wasn't sitting in judgment, and it was hard for him to believe in a love that wasn't dependent on circumstances.

Things didn't transition as quickly as I would have liked. For the next few weeks, Craig saw his therapist, continued living with Hannah, and also began spending a lot of family time with us. We'd go to the beach, to his family's country club, to baseball games. Friday night dinners together became a regular thing, and it all felt really good. Kane loved the time with us all together, and when he napped, it gave Craig and me the opportunity to have some real-life conversations about our next steps and about him coming home. We discussed how we could recover from this, we talked about my newly discovered spirituality, we talked about his fears about coming home, and we also started to dream together. I told him I wanted to move to Costa Rica and raise our kids on the beach. I pictured us swimming in the ocean together, our kids running around barefoot in the sand. This is something I had been envisioning since before I met Craig, but with our businesses, I never thought it would be possible. I wanted to live an unconventional life and raise our kids in unconventional ways. Craig was into it; he liked the dream. He asked why Costa Rica, and I said I didn't know, I just felt it.

During this conversation, I told him I didn't want him to move from her house to our condo. I wanted him to move back home with us. I didn't want us to pretend we needed to figure things out separately. I wanted to figure it out and heal together under the same roof. Him living in one place, me living in another felt like it's what we "should" do because I shouldn't be willing to just take him back. But I was. This is what I had been praying for, and I didn't want to keep delaying it.

I could see the relief in Craig's eyes as I shared this with him. It was the reassurance he'd been wanting. We both thought this would make things easier, but it didn't. Things were complicated, and over the next week or so, I could see him struggling, wavering back and forth, unsure what to do and what to choose. He was telling me what I wanted to hear and telling her what she wanted to hear.

I was very aware of this; she was not.

And to be honest, this isn't an accurate portrayal of what I felt was happening. He wasn't just telling us both what we wanted to hear, he kept bouncing back and forth in his own heart. He was speaking his truth, but his truth kept ping-ponging.

When he was with us, it was all he wanted, we were all he wanted, and he couldn't imagine moving forward any other way. And when he was with her, the coin would flip: she was what he wanted, and he couldn't imagine life without her. When he didn't see us for a few days, it was almost as if we'd stop existing in his world.

Fear was controlling him. He feared making the wrong decision, he feared being unhappy, he feared being left unwanted. And these fears paralyzed him.

It got to the point where we needed to have an honest conversation about her. The conversation was not what he expected. He expected me to say just leave her, leave her in the middle of the night like you left us. He expected me to think it should be easy, but I knew it wasn't.

I had stopped seeing her as the enemy. I saw her as a woman who had truly been there for him these past few months. She was there when he felt he had no one else to turn to, and that meant something. I felt grateful to her for that; while everyone else in his life was judging him and shaming him, she didn't. I knew she wasn't expecting what was about to come. She thought they were building a life together, and I didn't want her to feel what I felt when Craig walked out on me. I no longer wanted to see her in pain.

And I told him that, this time in a letter I actually sent to him, the first one he got to read.

> *This situation is hard ... really, really hard for all of us. You, me, and I'm sure Hannah too. And believe it or not, I don't want you to shatter her world. I know how that feels and I wouldn't wish it on anyone.*

I told him she deserved the truth.

> *It's okay to tell her you love her, but you also love me. I know in your head that it still seems "wrong" for you to love two people at once, but you do, and you don't need to deny that to either of us. Tell her the things that you have told me ... it's hard, but you're missing a whole piece of yourself and have been missing this piece for the past few months because you've been so caught up in the emotions of everything. You've been missing a HUGE part of you, and I sense that she knows this. She knows there is the part of you who is all about family, that you value your family, that you (in your own words) are a man who would die for his family. That is a big part of who you are!*

And I encouraged him to tell her the truth about how he was feeling about us.

> *You can tell her you aren't sure how things are going to work out between you and me because if we are being honest, I don't think you're really sure at this point. But like you've told me, tell her you need to sort it out, you want to try. You want Kane in your everyday life, and you want to be there when your daughter arrives.*

I asked him not to just walk out and leave her with no closure. I asked him to leave her with truth.

> I think she'll understand that; I think she's intuitively felt it. It's why she's been so afraid for us to spend any time together. I get it. I'm not saying this will be easy, and yes, I'm sure initially she will be angry and upset. But once those feelings die down, I think she will respect you for being honest and for providing her with this closure instead of just running away. I know that's how I would feel and how I'd want you to treat me.

I shared this letter with him, but I wasn't going to force anything. I trusted that he would figure it out, and I kept choosing what felt right for me. It worked for a little while, but there came the day that I stopped trusting and reverted back to control and manipulation.

I'm telling you, staying seated in the throne of the Goddess didn't come easily to me. I slipped back into victimhood many, many times, continuing to show God that the illusion of victimhood hadn't fully been dismantled for me (yet).

chapter 46 | god's hand

What if one day it all makes perfect sense? The things that feel unbearable in this moment, the pain, the suffering, the heartache, the fear, the disappointment.

What if you see that God has his hand in everything?

... the light.
... the love.
... the shadow.
... the darkness.
... life.
... death.

What if the fear you feel is the gateway to return to love? What if the anxiety is the invitation to come back home to yourself? What if the guilt shows you the thing you're ready to transcend? What if the shame highlights the judgments and untruths that you hold on to? Meaning you see where you judge, you see where you label things good/bad and right/wrong, and as you become aware of these untruths, you're led to ultimate truth.

Fear to Love.
Anxiety to Remembrance.
Guilt to Transcendence.
Shame to Truth.

What if the event, the situation, the experience is there to show you where you create limitations in your energy field?

And what if through the experience, you shatter any and all limitations of who you are and what you're here for?

Remembering that you are a child of God,
a child of the universe,
a child of nature.

And you are here to be the fullest expression of who you are as such.

chapter 47 | napa valley

Craig's birthday was coming up, and this is where my trust started to waver. For weeks, he'd repeatedly told me all he wanted for his birthday was his family back and a healthy daughter. But I also knew that two months prior, long before we had discussed reconciling, he had booked a trip for two to Napa for his birthday, and I was not the "plus one" on this ticket.

I kept waiting to see an email come through saying he'd canceled his flights, but as the date got closer and closer, I started questioning everything. With ten days left to go to his birthday, I just came right out and asked him about it. He was shocked, having no idea how I could even know about the trip, but he recovered quickly. He said it felt like it was forever ago he'd booked that trip and no, he wasn't going. He said he knew what he wanted in his life; he knew what was important and that was his family.

I let go of the breath I had been holding, but something didn't feel right. I had a feeling inside of me that I couldn't shake, but I shoved it down, wanting what he was saying to be true. He looked at me and told me not to worry, reminded me we were in a good place and that the war was over.

Kane and I went out of town for the next few days. This is when things would often fall apart, but this time they didn't. He seemed more convinced than ever that we were going to get through this together. He sent me listings of houses he thought we should buy. He was ready for a fresh start and thought we needed more room for the baby that would be arriving in just over a month.

There was one house in particular he was ready to put an offer on, but I told him he needed to slow down. I wasn't going to buy a new house, and kick off our fresh start, while he lived with another woman. That was a hard no.

But we kept talking, we kept exploring options, and I continued to check if he'd canceled his flights. He hadn't. And while it contradicted everything he had been saying, I knew he wouldn't. But again, I tried to will it to happen. I also contemplated canceling it for him; after all, I had access to his booking. It would be so easy to log on and just click that cancel button, but that came with the risk of starting World War III. So, I held off, giving Craig a chance to cancel on his own, to make the "right" decision. But when the flight was less than forty-eight hours away and it still hadn't been canceled, I asked again.

This time his response was he didn't know if he was going to go. He said he might just go since it was already booked and it would be a fun weekend away. All the peace, love, trust vibes I had been holding evaporated when I heard those words.

"A fun weekend away." Did he really just say that to me? We were exactly one month away from my due date, and all I'd been hearing was how desperately he wanted his family back. He'd just wanted us to buy a new house two days ago. What the actual f*ck was he thinking?

Did he truly think I should be okay with this? Did he truly think it wasn't a big deal that he was going away for one last weekend with his girlfriend before he broke up with her?

I started to question everything that had transpired over the month prior. Was it all a joke to him? Did any of it mean anything?

I pulled out all of the stops. I led with guilt, reminding him the doctors had warned us there was a high possibility that our baby girl would come early. I laid this on thick, saying I wouldn't be able to forgive him if he missed her birth. I questioned how he would ever forgive himself and asked him how he would explain it to her one day. When he said that was unlikely to happen, I told him that I had started to leak amniotic fluid, which was a bit of a stretch. The day before, I had feared I was leaking amniotic fluid, so I went to my midwife and they confirmed I wasn't. When that didn't seem to matter to him, I threatened him, saying that if he went I would see it as a sign that he was choosing his new life over his family, and that would be it for me. The ultimatum I said I wouldn't give, got dropped. I told him that if he went, I was closing down every door between us; there would be no chance of him and me reuniting. After six weeks of peace between us, this turned into another blowout, which ended with him again telling me I didn't control him.

I saw the patterns we played in. They were glaring me right in the face. This story was starting to feel very repetitive, the cycles of flowing *from Victim to Goddess, Victim to Goddess*, going around and around. Having a momentary breakthrough and then a complete breakdown. And because it was the only thing left for me to do, I surrendered.

I asked God to guide me, and I chose again. Choosing again in alignment with peace, choosing again in alignment with my soul's truth.

I went inward, asked for guidance, and came to the awareness that I needed to let Craig continue on his journey. This deeply pained me to admit. As much as I had held out hope over the past few weeks, he just wasn't there yet. My only choice was to release all the expectations I had placed on him. Yes, he had led us down that path, but it was up to me to release what wasn't serving me. And this entanglement with him was no longer serving me.

My man-made timeline wasn't serving me either. I had been telling everyone, including God, that I was willing to work this out between us, but only if he was home before our baby girl was born. This created more pressure for me and it's also where I showed God that I was buying into the illusion of limitation. I thought there was a limit and a timeline on my love and forgiveness. I thought there was a limit to what I could handle. I thought I didn't have the capacity to love or forgive beyond what my human could get behind.

When I look back in hindsight, this is how I picture God's reaction. I see his eyes smiling, I hear the chuckle in his voice, I sense the humor that he feels as he lovingly calls me out on the lies I tell myself.

He says, *Look at you. Look at how cute you are, dear child. Thinking that there are limitations in this world. Putting your timeline on things. It's cute. And it's not true. Let me show you. Let me show you that your love has no bounds. Let me show you that your timeline is creating a deadline, and that it's man-made. Let me show you the illusion you're buying into. Let me show you just how far from the truth you are.*

I knew I was living a lie. My feelings, my wants, my desires wouldn't disappear because a certain date, or a certain experience, had come and gone. That ultimatum I had given Craig was not laced in the frequency of truth, it was laced in the frequency of human manipulation. And that was no longer a life I was willing to live.

So, as hard as it was, I released my judgment and relinquished my desire to control what was happening. I stopped trying to speed up the ending of their relationship. I stopped fantasizing about forwarding her all of the texts that had been sent and photos that had been taken. I went deeper in trust, believing that there was something I wasn't seeing. And I sent out a prayer to whoever was there.

God, Angels, Spirit, I am willing to view this situation from a different lens. Show me a new perspective. Step in with the most peaceful, loving resolution for all of us.

Once I gave up control, it was easy to see how my anger, my frustration, and my attachment were blocking the flow between us. And so, I resorted to truth; it was all I had left.

I sent Craig another vulnerable email.

I've felt so scared thinking you going means you don't love us and you don't choose us, but I know that's not true. I know you just aren't there yet. So, I will just keep hoping and praying for the day that you are. I finally feel at peace with you going. I'm not sure why, but for some reason I feel you just need it. I want you to feel good again. I can see that you don't right now. It's so crazy; I wish I could describe it better to you, but it's a look in your eyes, it's this thing you do with your mouth . . . It hurts my heart and I don't even know if you recognize it in yourself.

I know you don't need my permission, but I just wanted to let you know I'm okay, Kane's okay. We are going to have a fun weekend! We love you and we will be here when you get back! Just the two of us. This baby girl will wait for you to come home. I already know she's a daddy's girl!

The moment I hit send, my phone rang. He couldn't have possibly read my email already. I debated picking up. I didn't have the energy for another fight, but I knew avoiding him wasn't the answer either, so I picked up and all he said was "Can I have Kane for my birthday Friday night?"

"I thought you were going to Napa?" I asked, confused.

"No, I canceled. I just want to spend the night with Kane. Is that okay?"

I said sure and didn't mention the email I had just sent him. He would read it soon enough. I hung up before he realized I was crying. I could feel God right there, in his beautiful, divine orchestration reminding me to have faith, telling me he's got this, he's got me, he's got Craig, and he's got our baby girl.

I understood in that moment that God enters when we are in full faith. When things looked the worst, when I thought we wouldn't survive this, and I found a way back to love, a way back to peace, well that's when the miracle unfolded.

As this understanding dropped in, I remembered another line from my favorite prayer: "Hold us in our suffering when we don't understand."

When we feel like it has taken forever for God to step in, it's because God is waiting for us . . . waiting for us to hand it over, to fully surrender.

To "Let Go and Let God."

chapter 48 | I surrender

There is surrender as an act and surrender as a complete letting go, an absolute faith, where there is no anticipation of outcome, no preferred destination, no doing it in order to get. This last one I've experienced as a controlled surrender, which is not truly surrender at all.

It's not a handover to God. It's not absolute faith. It's an attempt at spiritual manipulation, an attempt to control the energetics. But here's the thing: God cannot be deceived in this way. His language is the language of frequency, and frequency doesn't lie.

Letting Go and Letting God does not make you powerless.
It makes you powerful.

It represents your faith,
your trust,
your absolute knowing

that God is conspiring in your favor.

chapter 49 | the tide has two sides

On Craig's birthday, he came to pick up Kane, just like he had asked. But instead of going out the two of them, they stayed and we celebrated as a family, all three of us. Balloons, dinner, cupcakes, candles, all of it. Craig asked to spend the night again. It was so weird to hear him ask if he could sleep in our home. His birthday wish was to wake up together, as a family, and it was a wish I wanted to fulfill. I wanted to forget everything that had happened, and everything that was going on around us, even if it was just for a day, even if it was just for the night.

It felt good to go to sleep together, and it felt good to wake up together, in the simplicity of family life. The three of us spent the morning cuddled up in bed, reading books, telling stories, and giggling. Craig made Mickey Mouse pancakes, Kane's favorite, we ate, and he left.

Obviously, I knew where he was going, and who he was going to spend the rest of his birthday with, and I didn't care. It didn't actually matter to me, so I stopped making it mean anything. I didn't even entertain the thought of making it mean something. I didn't allow myself to spiral.

I told myself "it is what it is in this moment," knowing that at any moment things could change, the tides could shift. This was the best way forward for me. I didn't want to force the tides to shift; I didn't want Craig to end his relationship because I'd given him an ultimatum. I wanted to let it play out; I wanted to trust in the unfolding. So, I stopped questioning Craig, and I stopped questioning God. I stopped asking when, I stopped asking how, I stopped asking why not yet.

I just continued to move forward, choosing to live and to bring forth the Goddess energy I felt within me. Because this is what I truly felt.

I felt like a Goddess, which was much different than how I felt during my first pregnancy. For months I had been spending hours each week with an energy healer. Her space was called The Womb, and every time I went, it literally felt like I was being held in her womb.

She poured love over me, nurtured me, and we'd pray together and talk about God. She led me through sound-healing journeys. She was my baby whisperer. Each time I was there, my baby girl and I had a direct line of communication. She was speaking to me through my soul, saying, "Mama, don't worry about me. I'm going to make it; I'm going to hold on." I also often felt her telling me she was going to be a daddy's girl, and I believed her. This little soul growing inside me felt so wise. It felt like I was birthing through her as she was birthing through me.

For months I had also been meditating and praying multiple times a day. I listened to spiritual music and read spiritual texts. I spent time with girlfriends, having deep soul conversations. All of this was new to me. All of it was part of my journey *from Victim to Goddess*.

At this point, I felt the sexiest I had ever felt in my life, which I never would have imagined. This baby inside of me was the most powerful healing angel. I wanted to capture the feeling, so I asked a photographer friend to meet me in the park one day for a full photoshoot with Kane, my bump, and me. I was close to naked for most of the shoot. Kane's bare bum rested on my bare belly, and I felt truly happy in that moment.

Truly happy and truly free. I felt the presence of God within me and all around me. I remembered the words I felt at the beginning of this journey, that "I was going to be okay," and I started to realize I actually felt more than okay. I felt filled with faith, filled with love, filled with God. I knew that this entire journey, as hard as it was, filled with all of the ups, downs, and tidal waves—it had been a gift. An answer to a prayer I didn't pray for at the human level, but at the soul level.

This felt good. This was all that I needed; nothing else was required. I was reminded of the words "this or something better," and I felt what these words meant. This is enough and I'm available for more, I'm open to receive gifts from the universe, I trust in the divine dance. "This or something better" became a phrase I adopted into my meditations and prayers.

It had been a week since Craig's birthday. Kane and I were getting ready to leave town for a week at the beach. It would be our last trip out of the city, as my due date was exactly three weeks away. I was a little nervous heading so far out of the city this close to my due date, but my midwife said the fact that we made it to thirty-seven weeks without needing to induce was a miracle within itself, and at this point, we would allow her to come naturally. She assured me that this baby was nowhere close to being born. I obviously had an intuition, though, because I asked her what if—just in case. And so, we made a plan in case I went into labor.

The night before we left, Craig came to hang out with Kane and asked me to hang out with them. He'd brought takeout and thought we could have a night together like we did on his birthday, but I already had plans to meet up with a girlfriend and her new boyfriend. Craig tried to get me to bail on her, but I didn't want to. I was in my Goddess vibes, and I didn't want to give in to him because I thought it might alter the state in which I left for the beach the next morning.

I got home later than I typically did, and Craig wasn't downstairs. I assumed he and Kane had fallen asleep up in my bed. I wandered upstairs, thinking I'd switch spots with Craig, but when I got to the top of the stairs, I could see Kane fast asleep in his own bed. I walked farther down the hall and found Craig sleeping in my bed. I sat down beside him to wake him up, to tell him I was home and that he could get going, but he told me he didn't want to leave, he wanted to stay. And that dream I had been having, the sex one, it got played out in real life.

And just like my dreams foreshadowed, our sexual chemistry was undeniable. We made love in the most raw, passionate, intimate way. While we laid together afterward, he told me how much he has missed this, us together, our bodies knowing each other so well. I agreed as I fell asleep in his arms.

The next morning, he put both Kane and me in the car with three kisses: one for Kane, one for me, one for my belly. And he asked me to trust him. He didn't give me a date or a timeline, but he said he promised he would be back home before our baby girl was born. She would come into this world with her family together. This is what I had truly been praying for. How it unfolded didn't matter to me anymore.

chapter 50 | deeper in

If I trust in all that is, then what . . .
If I drop the questioning energy . . .
If I release the doubt . . .

If I believe in what I can't yet see . . .
If I know that I already know—not in my mind but in my soul.

If nothing is missing.
If I'm never disconnected, then what . . .

Then what do I know . . .
What do I feel . . .
What do I experience . . .

I experience that:

God is always there.
I'm always held.
I'm always being invited in.

Invited to go
Deeper in truth.
Deeper in divine wisdom.
Deeper in self.

I trust in all that is.
In ways seen and unseen.

Choosing to live, breathe, work, play, and express myself in the frequency my soul knows as home.

chapter 51 | sloan

Three days later, while at the beach with Kane, my sisters, and all of my nieces and nephews, I got the first message from Craig since we had left, asking what we were up to. I replied with a picture of Kane and me cuddled up on a beach chair.

These would be the last few moments when it was just him and me. In less than three weeks, his sister would arrive. I wanted to savor each and every moment. Craig must have felt this too. His response to the picture was that he didn't want to waste any more time, and he didn't want to miss out on making any more memories. He asked if he could come join us at the beach. He said he would end it with Hannah, move out of her place, and tomorrow would be a new beginning for our family. It was finally happening.

But Sloan decided not to wait. My midwife was wrong; my intuition was right. Two hours later, my water broke. We didn't get the chance for our final beach days together, and Craig didn't get the chance to end his relationship. When my water broke, he started to drive toward me, and my sister started to drive me toward him. We were all praying that we would find each other in time and that our baby girl wouldn't be born on the side of the highway.

She birthed through me, and I birthed through her. This is the experience I had with bringing my daughter into this world. As of twenty-eight weeks, the doctors evaluated me weekly with the expectation that they would very likely have to induce at any moment so she'd have a better chance of survival. To carry her to thirty-two weeks was the goal of my team. My goal was to carry her to thirty-seven weeks so I could have a natural water birth with my midwives. No one thought that would be possible.

But I knew. I knew the life force energy she and I had been breathing into each other.

At thirty-seven weeks and one day, I went into labor. For a long time, it had been unknown if my husband would be there for her birth. I had four girlfriends on call. They'd made a schedule, ensuring that every day one of them would be available for me so I didn't have to fear bringing this baby into the world alone. Even if Craig was going to be there, one of them would be there as well to support me. There was only one day in the last month before my due date they were all unavailable, and, of course, it was the day I went into labor. God was clearly showing me that Craig and I were meant to have this experience together, and alone.

As we were speeding down that highway, I acknowledged this, that this experience was meant to be him and me. I also prayed that it wouldn't just be him and me.

"Please, God, let us make it to the birthing center."

"Please, baby girl, hold on."

She held on, she waited for her daddy, and she waited until we got back to the city, but barely. We got to the birthing center, I made it into the bathtub, and then I told Craig he needed to get the midwife, who was in another room, and he needed to hurry.

As they came running into the room, I was already bringing our daughter into the world. Her and me, together. They witnessed me catch her under the water, then I handed her to my husband, he held her and then laid her back on my chest.

Sloan Alida Shaw. She was perfect in every way, perfectly healthy but tiny. We were so afraid for so long that she wasn't coming, that she wasn't here to stay. And then she arrived, becoming the reason Craig believes in angels.

PART THREE

the second smackdown

"THOSE WHO ARE
CERTAIN OF THE
OUTCOME CAN AFFORD
TO WAIT, AND WAIT
WITHOUT ANXIETY."

–A COURSE IN MIRACLES

chapter 52 | trust

What if the most radical form of trust is not needing to trust at all but it's understanding that all is because it is. God is always there. God is always conspiring in your favor. Love is always available.

Your prayer is answered the moment you pray for it. The moment you command it, you choose it with your own free will. And this is the moment heaven and earth start shifting to bring it, the thing you've commanded forth into existence.

To trust in this, it's about knowing it exists in quantum form first. And then the action/non-action you take, the control vs. the surrender, the requirement vs. the allowance, determines when, if, and how rapidly you experience it here on earth, in the physical realm.

The problem is, many people don't believe in its existence. It being the desire, the answered prayer, until it is manifested in the human realm. "You have to see it to believe it" needs to be replaced with "You have to believe it to see it." And I would take this even deeper here . . . you have to know it to experience it.

You have to know at a human level, in your consciousness, that it already exists just beyond what your human eye can see. You have to know at a soul level it exists because you exist. It is designed uniquely for you.

You have to know that your energy field is what calls it forth, magnetizing it into reality, into physical form.

The prayer responds to your energy field.
The desire responds to your energy field.
The love responds to your energy field.
The money responds to your energy field.

The truth responds to your energy field.

God responds to your energy.
You set the stage.
You determine where God meets you.
You invite God to play.

It's not about controlling God and the desire,
controlling God and love,
controlling God and money,
controlling God and truth.

It's about commanding God, in unity. You and God as one. Bringing your soul desires forth. Believing in all that is. Allowing the truth to vibrate through your being. With a decision to know and experience yourself as the creator that you are.

chapter 53 | shaky ground

Craig came home with us that morning, the morning of Sloan's birth, and told me he was there to stay. I felt a sigh of relief, because up until he said those words, I truly wasn't sure.

I went into labor before anything had been resolved between him and her, and I had no idea what that meant. But for the next week he was home, he took the week off work, and just like he had done when Kane was born, he took care of me so I could take care of Sloan. He was on full-time Daddy duty: feeding, making bottles, changing diapers. When Sloan would wake up in the middle of the night, he'd bring her to me.

This is when we started playing house, pretending we were this perfect little family of four. We captured the picture-perfect moments to share on social media. Everyone congratulated us, telling us how blessed we were and what a perfect family we had. "The million-dollar family," they said. We could stop, we had it all.

I say we were playing house because that's what it felt like. Craig was sleeping on the couch but assuring me that his relationship was done. He pretended that he wasn't seeing Hannah, and I pretended to believe him, even though I knew that he was.

After everything I had shifted over the past six months, it felt like I was right back at the beginning. All of the spiritual work I had done was put on the back burner. All the opening, releasing, surrendering, and here I was, willing to bottle my feelings back up. We weren't discussing anything that had happened the past six months; we weren't discussing how we were going to move forward. I had no idea what he was telling her, but I knew they weren't done.

We were tiptoeing around each other. It didn't feel good, but we both became good at pretending it did. We did all the things we thought a family was supposed to do. We went for walks in the park, we spent time with our families, we went to my nephew's hockey games. Craig was home, Sloan was healthy, and Kane was obsessed with his baby sister.

This was what I had prayed for; this was what I wanted. God handed it over on a silver platter. But it didn't feel the way I expected it to feel, and I felt so guilty for feeling that way, for feeling like it wasn't enough.

I told myself I should be so incredibly grateful. God delivered on the timeline I had said things needed to happen by. Craig needed to be home by Sloan's birth, and he was. Who was I to feel like this wasn't the way it was supposed to be? It was exactly what I had asked for. "Ask and it is given" perfectly played out. And so, because of this, I didn't share my feelings of unease; I didn't share how messed up everything felt. I didn't share and Craig didn't share. He bottled everything up as well. Night and day, we danced around each other in our home. And I felt more lost with him being there than I had when he wasn't.

Things were definitely weird between us, but they were weirder between him and her. When Sloan was a week old, he told me he needed the one night he didn't have the day she was born to end things for good.

I gave him that night, but then the next day he retracted and said I misunderstood. The day after that, he retracted his retraction, saying, "I don't know what's the matter with me. I'm a horrible husband and horrible father. I don't mean to hurt anyone. I love you three more than anything. I hope one day you can forgive me."

This was the day he was in the darkest place I had ever seen him, and it was only about to get worse. The next part of the story is not my story to tell, and so I won't. She doesn't deserve that. This is the day they broke up, he packed up his stuff from her house, and after the events that ensued that night, I was certain he would never entertain the thought of going back there. He knew there was no way me or his family would allow her to meet our kids.

For a few days they didn't have contact, and then he reached out to her. I saw the email he sent. I expected this to happen, but I definitely didn't think he would be the one initiating it. They planned to meet up "just to talk." And instead of confronting him about it, I reverted back to tactics of manipulation and control.

I had a battle going on within myself. I wanted to have faith, but I didn't want to get blindsided again. I was feeling too vulnerable. I knew the where and the when they were meeting, so I stationed my girlfriend directly on their pathway to catch him in this lie.

My girlfriend played her part well, approaching him on the street and asking how the kids and I were doing. The fact that he stopped to talk to her with Hannah by his side made it seem like he was making a choice. He knew she would tell me. He knew I would know he had lied about seeing Hannah. I expected that to be it. I didn't expect him to return home that night, and I was surprised when he did.

As he came in, he sat beside me on the couch and took my hand in his, telling me, "It's over for good now. We needed closure. She's out of our life."

I took a deep exhale, letting the weight of everything I had been holding onto—the fear, the worry, the anxiety—leave my body. I didn't have the desire to prod any further or question him more. I was ready for it to be done. To close the chapter on her.

Another week went by, and again, they had no contact. But that didn't really seem to mean anything; we barely had contact either. We were living in the same house and avoiding each other as much as possible.

We had a three-week old baby, and figuring out how to heal together felt complicated. Neither of us knew where to begin. I could feel the pain he was sitting in. I could sense his confusion. I wanted to help him process it all, but I didn't know how. I booked an appointment for us to talk to a relationship therapist, but then canceled it. I didn't think he was ready, and I was afraid that if I pushed him to talk, he would shut down even further. So, I let him be on his own, hoping that he was sorting things out for himself and not realizing how isolating this was for him.

My emotions were yo-yo-ing all over the place. I would open my mouth to speak, I would reach my arm out to touch him, and then I would pull back. And then I'd feel the pull to reach out to him again. I knew we couldn't keep going like this; I couldn't keep going like this; neither of us would survive. We had to start communicating. We needed to have real, honest conversations. And so, finally, after a few more days, I initiated the first conversation with softness and tenderness:

"Do you miss her?"

"I don't miss her. But there are parts of that life that I miss. Especially because of how it's feeling here."

"Because of how uncomfortable it is between us?"

"Yeah."

"What was it like there?"

"It was easy. I didn't need to deal with any of this . . . with any of the mess I made. It was easy not having any responsibilities and drinking every night to bury my feelings. And there, no one judged me or cared about the choices I made. It made it easier for me not to care."

"Is it harder here because I care or because you don't think I care?"

"It's harder here because I care. I want our family so badly. I want to be here. I can't imagine not being here, but I don't even know what to do here. I don't know if I should talk to you. If I can hold you. If I can just be your husband. So, I sit here and think about what I should do and then just do what I can to help with the kids because I know how to do that. I know how to be a dad."

"What do you want with me? How do you want us to be together? Do you want to talk? Do you want to hold me?"

"It feels good talking now."

"So, just talk. Let's stop overthinking it and just talk. I can't keep holding back either. I can't keep telling myself we need more time. More time is creating more distance. I want you here with us. I want to support you. I always wanted to be here for you, even when you didn't want me to be."

"I know. Now that I'm not living the life that I was, I see things a lot differently. I see how destructive all of it was; I see how destructive that relationship was. I don't know what to say to you because you always saw it, and now I just feel stupid. How could I not see it when I was in it? Clearly Hannah didn't have my best interest in mind, even though she said she did. I always felt torn between her and Kane. If she really loved me, why would she try to stop me from seeing him? Wouldn't she encourage me to see him any chance I could? And every time you and I interacted, she told me you were manipulating me and I believed her . . . but now I see that she was the one manipulating everything."

"I'm sure she was scared of you leaving her. She knows how your relationship started. Kane and I were always a threat to your relationship with her; of course she didn't want you to spend time with us. You have to see that."

"I know. But then all the things she said about you. All the things I said about you. I don't know what to do about that now."

I took a deep breath and got honest. "She's not wrong. There were definitely a lot of moments when I tried to manipulate things and tried to manipulate you, especially in the beginning. My moves were very calculated. There were a lot of times I tested you and set you up for failure, and there were also a lot of times you thought I was and I truly wasn't. There were a lot of times I was trying to create peace between us."

"I know."

"And even when my actions didn't show it, I always had your best interest in mind. And I still do."

"Jak, I feel so f*cked up about this. I know what I want. I know my family is the only thing that matters to me. I just don't know how to move forward. I don't know how to live with you after what I've done to you."

"I don't feel the same way you do. I don't feel like you've done something to me, not anymore. Remember what I said to you in the car after my gramma's funeral?"

"I know, but I just don't get it. I've caused so much hurt and pain to you and everyone."

"I don't care about anyone else. I care about us. And I don't need to forgive you, that's already done, but you're going to have to find a way to forgive yourself."

We both fell silent. The conversation wasn't easy, but it was honest. And while we were done for the night and it was time to put the kids to bed, we promised to keep talking to each other. We both agreed it felt good.

chapter 54 | "it's nothing"

The next night I went to yoga. It was the first time Craig was alone with the kids since Sloan was born. I was gone for two hours. When I got home, he was in a bad place. The kids were fine, but he was not. His eyes were red. I could tell he'd been crying.

When I asked, he denied that anything was wrong and said he was good. I was annoyed. The day before he'd been so open to talk, and then that night, he became closed off. I went to bed frustrated. and then woke up at 5 a.m. to the sound of Craig in the shower. This was completely normal; he was getting ready for work. But something felt off. I could feel it inside me again, that voice urging me to listen. His phone was sitting right there beside me. I picked it up, typed in his passcode and saw the message he sent her after I went to bed.

It had been ten days since they had last spoken, ten days from the night when he told me he got his closure, ten days of no contact and then a text from him to her that read: "We need to talk. Can I come over tomorrow morning?" She said yes, and he said he'd be there at six.

When he got out of the shower, I asked him if something was up. I didn't want him to know I knew his passcode for his phone, so I told him I had this weird feeling about the day. I reminded him how strong my intuition was, but he told me nothing was up and to go back to sleep. I decided to be direct even if it got me caught.

I asked him if he was going to see her. He said no, why would I think that? I just reiterated what I said earlier, intuition, and left it at that.

After he left, I picked up my phone, then put it back down multiple times, wavering on what to do. Ultimately, I decided to pick it up and called a girlfriend who lived in the condo building beside Hannah's house. I asked her to go outside and take a picture of Craig's truck that I knew would be parked outside her house.

I was collecting evidence so Craig wouldn't be able to deny it, but I also wasn't prepared to do anything with this evidence, not yet. I wasn't ready to bring the truth I knew in my soul into my human reality. My soul and my mind were battling.

My soul was screaming that he was getting ready to leave again, but my mind couldn't believe it, not after the way things had ended between them.

I wanted this part of the story to be solid. I wanted to trust that God was giving me what I had been asking for the past seven months: my family together.

So, later, when he came home from work, acting as if everything was normal, I pretended it was too. I didn't wave the picture of his truck at her house in front of his face. I didn't even ask him. I shoved my soul-knowing down because my human self didn't want to face it. Even when he told me he was going to hockey and he'd be home after, I kept pretending to believe him. I tried to convince myself that it made sense. It was a Wednesday night, his regular hockey night, the first game of the season.

But I knew.
I couldn't convince myself.
He didn't even have his hockey equipment.

I let him leave with words unspoken between us. I knew I was watching him walk back into her life, and I didn't try to stop him because I kept hoping if I didn't say it out loud, it somehow wouldn't be true.

The next time I heard from him was 7 a.m. the following day. He sent a text and all it said was "I didn't want to wake you. The car is in the garage so you can take Kane to school."

There was no explanation as to why he didn't come home the night before, and when I asked, he said he had crashed at a buddy's after hockey.

I was pissed that we were back there again. Back to the lies.

I asked him if he was leaving us again, if he was going back to her. When he said no, I sent him the photo of his truck parked at her house so that he'd know I knew exactly what was going on.

He reiterated that it was nothing. And I lost it.

Him seeing her was not nothing. I couldn't believe that after two months of him telling me all he wanted was his family back, this was where we were. After he told me he resented her for all the times she asked him to choose between her and his son. After the thing I'm not even willing to speak of.

There I was, at home with our three-week-old daughter, our two-and-a-half-year-old son, and he was running around the city doing whatever he wanted.

I drove to his work to confront him face-to-face. I threatened to tell Hannah about everything that had been going on between us, about how for the month before Sloan was born he kept telling me all he wanted was his family back and he wanted to come home. About all the time we spent together, about the house he wanted us to buy, about the sex.

Once I put these threats between us, he didn't lie to me anymore. His anger began to match mine. First, he said she'd think I was crazy and wouldn't believe me. This is when I reminded him of all the texts he had sent me and the photos we had taken. I had a whole lot of proof.

He said it would ruin his life. It would destroy our relationship and his relationship with our kids if I did what I was threatening to do.

"No," I said. "You did that when you made the stupid f*cking choice you just made and decided to walk out on us, again."

The more we talked, the more we yelled, the more anger and hurt we both felt.

Until Craig attempted to bring peace between us. He looked at me with both pain and sincerity in his eyes. I felt the peace he was attempting to bring deep in my soul as he told me this was not how he wanted us to move forward, he didn't want to go back to the place we were at last spring where there was so much anger and hatred. He wanted us to work this out. He wasn't walking out on us.

I felt the truth in the words he had just spoken and in the words that came next.

"I want to live at home with you, but I might not come home every night."

Deep breath.

"I need to figure this out for myself. Yes, I was with Hannah. I'm not sure if she will be in my life forever, but I'm not ready to let her go. I need you to let me figure this out on my own."

I didn't agree, but he said he'd be home in an hour so we could talk. An hour went by, two hours went by, three hours went by, and then I got a text that read: "I don't think it's a good idea for me to be around you guys right now."

Feeling numb, I sent him a text back that said, "Fight for us, when you say you love us, fight. Don't believe the story you've told yourself that you can't recover from this, that it means something deeper, that it's f*cked up you could do this. It doesn't have to be this way, but you're going to have to choose it. I can't do it for you."

And that was it.

chapter 55 | abandonment

I woke up to an email the next morning sent from Craig to both his mom and me, and there was a bcc to Hannah that I wasn't supposed to know about. It was a long email in which Craig expressed that he was sorry he gave us both false hope on restoring our marriage. He said the things he said to me about wanting his family back and the texts he sent about resenting Hannah were said when he was at the lowest point in his life.

He said he couldn't live at home anymore because he'd come to realize how truly manipulative I was, and he urged his mother to see it too. He said one day he might wake up and realize that everyone around him was right, but it's not how he felt that day. He said he reached out to Hannah because he missed her and wanted her by his side in whatever happened next. Even if that meant I would take our kids away from him. And he signed it off: "So that's it. I guess whatever happens next, happens."

So much for him not wanting to go down the same pathway we had previously gone down.

I was done.

I had a three-week old baby and a two-and-a-half-year-old child. I couldn't be there to navigate this with him any longer. I wasn't going to continue to choose this for any of us. We had sold our house two weeks before when Sloan was just a week old so we could have a fresh start. Our moving day was still a month away, but I packed up everything I could fit into our car and we left.

I wasn't attempting to deprive him of us like I had done before with the hope he would wake up. I just didn't have it left in me to fight, and I wasn't going to continue to live two blocks away from him so it was easier on him. I chose what was easier on me. I decided to move to my mom's house.

It was easier and harder at the same time. I knew once I landed there, it would be easier, and I would have the support I needed. We would be two hours outside of the city, close enough for Craig to come see the kids whenever he wanted, but far enough away that I wouldn't have to relive the nightmare of him and her again. The drive to get there was excruciating, though. I felt like I was dying. I shed a million tears on that drive, and not for me this time, but for him.

I felt like I was abandoning him. In the time when I knew he needed to be loved, I was leaving.

When I shared these feelings with his mom, she said, "Jak, you're not abandoning him, he abandoned you."

She didn't get it. Of course she would only see it that way; this was how everyone saw it. And I got it. I knew this was what it looked like, but that's not what it felt like. I saw his hurt, and I saw how lost he was. I felt his pain and saw how he was choosing to numb it. I had heard his truth the night before he left for the second time, and I knew this truth was his deepest truth. He told me how scared he was. He told me he feared not being needed and being abandoned. He had themes of abandonment running through his whole life, and there I was, leaving him behind. Letting that theme of abandonment continue to stay present for him.

I wanted to shake him so he'd wake up. I didn't want him to slip back into this darkness. Who would want that for the person they loved or the father of their children? Not me. I wanted to save him from himself, but I couldn't. I wasn't supposed to. I had to remind myself this was his journey, not mine.

And I reminded myself of something one of my soul sisters said after the first tidal wave hit. She told me I couldn't rob Craig of his bottom. Meaning he might not be open to rise, to see truth until he hit his rock bottom.

God, all I wanted to do was pull him out, to stop him from the negative cycle, but I knew I couldn't. I couldn't try to make sure he would avoid hitting that place. I needed to let him go, for him as much as for me and the kids. By letting him go, by letting him hit rock bottom, I trusted that he would find the light. Craig himself had said to me that he didn't know if Hannah would be in his life forever. But he knew right then that it was where he wanted to be, and he asked me to let him figure it out on his own.

All I could choose in that moment was to return to love. I prayed to my angels to carry my peace and loving vibes to him, and I chose to let go.

chapter 56 | lead me in love

God, lead me in love.

In everything I do.
In who I am.
In the words I speak.
In the energy I bring forth.

Love is my religion.
Devotion is my language.

Guide me to lead with love.

chapter 57 | discernment

We had been with my family for four days and I hadn't heard a word from Craig. Not a "did we make it safe" text, not a check-in on his kids, nothing. I went to visit a family friend who is also a medium. She was worried about me and told me that I needed to separate myself as far as possible from Craig.

She said, "He is in a deep, dark place. The angels can't reach him; he is too far gone."

These messages shocked me. They didn't feel correct. They just didn't sit right with me. These messages instilled fear not faith; they didn't feel God-given. God doesn't operate in the frequency of fear, he operates in the frequency of love.

So, I was left with two questions: What was I going to be willing to believe in that moment? Would I let fear take over or go deeper in faith? I went deeper in truth. I sat with myself and asked myself what felt true to me, and the truth is, I had stopped believing in that type of God months before.

I had stopped believing in good or bad, right or wrong.
I had stopped believing that God punishes and condemns.

I didn't believe it was possible to ever be "too far gone." No matter who you are and what you've done, there is always a pathway to God. God is available to all of us at any moment in time. Love is always available at any moment it time, we just need to choose it.

The angels, spirit, God, they hadn't turned their back on Craig. It's true he may have chosen not to be available to listen, but God wasn't leaving him. God would be there patiently waiting for Craig to see the love within himself. This I knew. I felt it so deeply within me. I wasn't willing to waver in that truth, in the knowing that God is always there, always in all the ways.

Knowing this, I had a choice to make once again.

I could go back to being the victim. I could give God the middle finger and turn my back on him and everything I had embodied over the past seven months. I could blame him for giving me what I wanted and taking it away again.

Or I could go deeper in everything I had remembered about who I am and who we all are.

I could go

deeper in love.
deeper in surrender.
deeper in peace.
deeper in faith.
deeper in forgiveness.

I could let go and let God.

I could trust the universe was conspiring in my favor. I could continue to believe there were things happening beyond what I could see with my human eyes. I could have faith that this was all in service of my soul's agenda.

And that's exactly what I chose to do.

Once again choosing my soul's truth over anything else.

Choosing to rise as the Goddess.

This is when my belief in myself became stronger than any other belief I held. This is when I fully attuned to the knowing that God lives within me, as he lives within you.

Why would I believe in anything or anyone else more than my own inner wisdom? Why do you?

It's time to fully shift the paradigm. And it's time to fully shift the ways of operating where you think someone else knows better than you.

We, as humans, have been telling ourselves this lie for far too long.

It stops right here.
Right now.

"*I TELL YOU THIS:*
COMPASSION NEVER ENDS,
LOVE NEVER STOPS,
PATIENCE NEVER RUNS OUT
IN GOD'S WORLD.
ONLY IN THE WORLD OF MAN
IS GOODNESS LIMITED.
IN MY WORLD,
GOODNESS IS ENDLESS."

–NEALE DONALD WALSCH

chapter 58 | too far gone

We are never too far gone. We are never in a place or a state of being where love can't reach us, where God can't reach us.

For we are love.
And God resides within us.

God is not an almighty power you need to seek to find outside of you, "seek and you shall find" means seek within.

Within you find love.
Within you find God.

From the seat of the victim, it would have been easy for me to believe Craig was too far gone. It would have given me validation. It would have given me permission to respond in rage, to walk away from that which I knew to be true. It would have given me permission to paint him as the bad guy and to make choices for me and my kids within this narrative that would have been chosen in hatred, not love.

Can you see how this narrative would have greatly impacted what came next? It would have closed down the invitation for Craig to choose to heal within our family. It would have pushed him further out, further away from the remembrance of who he is. And ultimately, I believe it would have led him to a place of taking zero self-responsibility whatsoever.

That's what the victim/villain scenario provides us.

If I am the victim, I do not have to take personal responsibility for anything. "Poor me."

If I am the villain, I get to say, "It's just who I am."

But when I'm neither the victim nor the villain, this is where I get to take radical responsibility for what comes next. For what I create in response to life. For what I create with my thoughts, my words, my actions, and my reactions.

If I am not the villain or the victim, then who am I?
I am who I am.
I am the Truth.

And within this truth, I become willing to see the illusions I've bought into:

The illusion of victimhood.
The illusion of fear.
The illusion of sacrifice.

If it's all an illusion, then what?

Then we become willing to see that it's all designed to be transcended.

Fear that you won't have enough, that you aren't enough, that you aren't worthy or deserving enough. These are all illusions. Nothing makes you worthy or deserving. You are worthy simply because you are.

As humans, we love to complicate almost everything, especially our worthiness and our enoughness. We create all sorts of wild formulas in regard to what we need to do in order to receive. We don't allow for it to be simple.

"Ask, and it shall be given."
"Knock, and the door will open."

We tell ourselves, no! That can't be true, it can't be that simple!

Why don't we want to believe it can be this easy? Because it would highlight many things within our human experience that we have been ignoring for centuries. It would show us that things don't have to be the way they've always been, the way we've always experienced them to be.

That life doesn't have to be hard.
It doesn't have to be a struggle.
It doesn't have to be based on sacrifice and compromise.

This is how we create a new way forward, by deciding things don't need to be experienced the way they've been experienced before; this is what creates true liberation. It creates ultimate freedom for who we are individually and collectively as creators.

All we have to do is take radical responsibility for that which we create. But that, right there, is what often limits us from taking radical responsibility as the creators of life itself. Understanding that all exists because you exist. Because you have created it.

It can feel safer to not "know" this. It can feel more comfortable, that's for sure. Because what happens when we understand this and look back in hindsight is that we see that we never had to suffer. We never had to take the long road or the hard road. We never had to sacrifice. We never had to choose one or the other.

These can be some hard truths to face as we move into this deeper spiritual awareness.

If it's all an illusion, then our suffering, our sacrifice, our uphill battle, no longer feel worth it. They're not validated. So, you see it can serve us to not know, to not remember, to not see. It can serve us to protect our human self from these truths. Because it allows us to remain living within the illusory world.

But you know as you read this, it does not truly serve you in any way, shape, or form, not at a soul level. Your non-remembrance only serves you if you choose to remain in the illusion of ignorance. Ignorance, shame, guilt, and regret are feelings that may come up for you as you go deeper in your remembrance. This is where I invite you to remember that you did not know then what you know now. You are not who you were then. You were not in the state of awareness that you are in, in this very moment.

You are here on a journey of the growth and evolution of your soul.

You are not the same person you were five seconds ago.
Five minutes ago.
Five weeks ago.
Five months ago.
Five years ago.

With each new moment of remembrance, the energetic composition shifts. There is no shame in the fact that there are things you've forgotten on this journey, you've simply forgotten so that you can remember and so that you can deepen in your remembrance. Celebrate that. Celebrate that the forgetting has led you here, has led you in remembrance.

Remembrance of who you are and why you're here. Remembrance that you are the creator. You are the one. You and God are one. Your wants and God's wants are the same. There is nothing that you could want that God does not want for you. God is not here to limit you, to judge you, to have you sacrifice for him.

God is here to experience life moving through you, love moving through you, truth moving through you. So, go out and live. Experience life. Love from the depth of your soul. Don't attach your love to anything.

Give love freely. Receive love freely. Stand in your truth. Speak your truth. Move in alignment from the truth within you.

You are here to be the fullest expression of all that you are. Go out into the world and show off. Show us your magnificence, and your uniqueness. Share your medicine, your voice, and your sacred wisdom with us.

The world needs all of you.
All of me.
All of us.

ALL EXISTS
BECAUSE
YOU EXIST.

chapter 59 | the answer to your prayer

You're the creator.

Tune into the God within.
Tune into the sacred wisdom within.

And bring it forth from the depth of your knowing, the depth of your truth.

Power does not reside outside of you.
Truth does not reside outside of you.

God is Godding from within you.

All exists in frequency first.
You are the answer to someone else's prayer.
Act accordingly.

chapter 60 | this is for you

After the session with the family friend/medium, I took my baby girl for a walk in the park. I sat by the river as she slept beside me. I opened up my journal and wrote the words that had just come through.

> *The first time he left, it was for me. The second time he left, it was*
>
> *for you.*

You meaning you, the person who is reading this right now. I knew in that moment, this book would be written. I knew that this story, this journey *from Victim to Goddess*, was meant to be shared.

I didn't know what was going to happen next. I didn't know the way in which things would unfold. But I knew a few things.

I knew God never gives us something we can't handle.

I knew we had a choice in everything.

I knew we get to choose what we make anything mean.

I knew every human experience we have serves the agenda of our soul.

CAN I BE
THE VOICE
OF TRUTH
THAT RUNS
THROUGH ME?

chapter 61 | you have what it takes

What if you knew this is what's it's all about
. . . bringing your truth forward.

That's it.

It's about
. . . leading with truth.
. . . speaking your truth.
. . . being your truth.

Without interference.
Without need or requirement.
Without buying into any of the illusions.
Without creating formulas.
Without trying to predict what comes next.

You as the creator.
You as the vessel of God.
You as the voice of the truth that runs through you.

It's truly that simple.
I promise.

Your truth is your medicine, and your medicine is magic.

You're so much more capable than you give yourself credit for. You
have what it takes. You have the ability to hold much more than you
know right now. Your soul is screaming for new levels of freedom.
New portals of expansion. New depths of expression.

Deep inside, you know it. Your lived experiences, your sacred
wisdom, and the truth you hold inside of you is beyond valuable. It
is beyond needed in this world. It is meant to be shared.

chapter 62 | I wanted vengeance

Another week went by. Another week without hearing from Craig, and I asked myself if we were finally at the point in our journey where it would actually end. Seven months prior, when it all began, I knew our journey wasn't over. I tried to make sense of all that had happened since.

Maybe we were meant to come back together just for the birth of our daughter. Maybe it was my holding on that was prolonging the inevitable end.

I still didn't think so, though. I still thought our story would continue, but I also felt it sounded insane to say. The rational part of me, my mind, said, *Are you crazy? Your marriage is over, your husband has left not once, but twice. Your baby girl is a month old, he's gone, your marriage is gone.*

His family told me I needed to move on, for myself, and for the kids. They said they would do all they could to support me, but I needed to let go.

My spiritual self kept telling me something different, though. And that voice within me started to guide me in a different direction. The whispers sounded like this: "Stop trying to force your family together. The forcing keeps leading to the same result. Craig pulls further away and shuts his emotions down."

I was confused.

Was I supposed to let go? To hold on?

All I knew was the forcing had to stop, and I reminded myself to allow the unfolding.

I told God it was all his.

I was ready to remove my hands from the steering wheel and move forward in my own life. I continued to send Craig and Hannah peace through prayers. I spent my days out in nature with my babies. I went deep in my spiritual practices. I launched my first course into the world: The Spirit Course. I served God, and I allowed God to serve me. I was surrounded by the people I love most. And I felt good. I felt like a Goddess, most of the time.

But then one night, I wavered. I heard from someone from Craig's past, and within that conversation, I let feelings of hurt, anger, and jealousy take over. I engaged in the drama of my situation. I shared things that shouldn't have been shared, that weren't my story to tell. And as I was caught up in this energy, I opened my computer to check up on him.

I had finally deleted his email off my computer, but I remembered I could still check his credit card transactions. I held my baby girl in my arms and told myself to stop. I pleaded with myself to delete his account just like I deleted his email. I told myself this wouldn't be good for any of us. But ultimately, I didn't listen. I checked his credit card statement and saw what looked like two one-way flights to Australia. I thought to myself, he's really doing it.

I told my mom, and she said, "Jaclyn, you don't know this for sure."

"Yes, I do." I replied.

I didn't sleep that night, and by the time morning came, I was ready to fully unleash on Craig.

I sent off texts in rapid fire. First asking if he was ever going to ask about his kids who he hadn't checked in on or seen for almost two weeks. I told him he was a deadbeat father and a lousy example of a man.

He fired back and said he didn't want me to contact him again and that, going forward, he would only communicate with me through our lawyers.

I said I had no desire to communicate at all. I told him we didn't want him. We didn't need him, and we were better off without him. I also said I knew about his tickets to Australia. And told him to have a nice f*cking life living across the world from his children.

He said he needed to get as far away from me as he could so that he could live a nice f*cking life and finished the conversation by telling me he was never coming back.

And that was it. There was no fight left within me.

I told him my lawyer would send him the paperwork so he could hand over sole custody of our children. I was DONE.

chapter 63 | failing

You'll fall. You'll fail.

Sometimes in small ways.

Sometimes in big ways.

It's part of the initiation.
It's part of the journey.

And it's the part I care least about.
I care about what you do after.

I care about you getting back out in that water.
I care about your bravery and your willingness.

I care that you lean in for the full human experience.
I care that you keep going.

Leading, moving, choosing from the frequency of truth.

chapter 64 | I lost myself

I lost myself in those twelve hours. I forgot who I was. I forgot who we all were. I forgot to lead with love.

But I decided not to punish myself for it because I had this thought: *What if the forgetting exists simply to lead to a more potent remembering?*

The forgetting of who we are creates the remembering of who we are.

So, the forgetting is actually a gift, as it leads to the remembrance of the power we hold. To the remembrance that we are the cocreators of our existence. To the remembrance that we are heaven in human form.

The forgetting is human nature. And the forgetting, followed by the remembering, allows us to deepen our embodied wisdom. It provides us with an opportunity to expand our energetic field.

So, we don't need to worry when we forget who we are or how powerful we are. We don't need to worry if we've allowed our light to be dimmed or our voice to be dulled.

It doesn't matter.
That doesn't determine what happens next.

Right now matters.
What you choose in this moment matters.

Choose to remember.

If you feel lost, find yourself.

chapter 65 | I found myself

I went for a walk in the park with my mom and our kids. But as soon as we got there, I told her I needed to be alone. She went off with them and I sat by myself, just me and me. I sat with the day's events and asked myself if the words I had spoken were really true.

Did I believe we were better off without Craig?
Was I finally done?
Had we exhausted all options together and was I ready to close the door forever?

I also got really curious with myself.
What had I been fighting for all of this time? Why had I truly been fighting?

Had I continued to feel the soul nudge that our story wasn't over?
Or at some point did my human take over and just want to win?

This felt like a big question. Did I want Craig and me together, or did I just not want them together? Was I doing all this just to say I won, he chose me?

I asked myself these questions, but I didn't really need to. I knew the why for me. It had nothing to do with winning and everything to do with trusting what I felt inside.

And so once again, I let myself choose. This time, closing the gap in the timeline. It had been two hours since the last messages I sent Craig, the ones not expressed in the frequency of truth. The last message between us was the one he'd sent.

I chose to shift the frequency between us, once again choosing to express the truth that felt so vulnerable to share.

"I don't think we are better off without you. The kids are definitely not better off without you. And I don't believe you are better off without our kids.

"I'm scared for you. I'm scared that one day you will wake up on the other side of the world and you won't recognize yourself. I think you will be miserable living a life without our kids, and I don't want that for you or for them.

"I saw you struggling the three weeks you were home, and it was hard to witness. I don't want more of that in your future. I want you to heal. I want our kids to experience the love that you exude so easily. I am dropping the hope for us, but I will hold the hope for you and our kids. And if you ever wake up on the other side of the world and feel alone, the kids and I will be here. We won't wait for you, but we will be here."

As the tears fell from my face, I turned off my phone. I prayed for peace between Craig and me, and I laid down to meditate.

An hour later, I turned my phone back on and saw the flood of messages that had come in from Craig. The first message said he was only going to Australia for a two-week vacation; he said he would never leave the three of us behind. He told me to do whatever I needed to do for me and the kids, and he would always figure out a way to make it work so that he could be in their life.

I could feel him spiraling, starting to question everything again, wondering how we got back to this place.

And then the last message: "In those three weeks when you saw me struggling, when you knew I was lying, when you knew I felt all alone, why didn't you say anything?"

I told him I didn't say anything because I didn't know what to say. Everything felt so fragile.

When Sloan came early, he just came home with us and there was no time to adjust. I had felt just as lost as he did. Like him, I tried to pretend everything was normal while walking on eggshells all day long.

One moment he would seem so happy to be there with us, and the next he'd seem so distant. I told him I'd booked an appointment for us to talk to a therapist together, but then canceled it, thinking he wasn't ready for that, worried I was forcing and pushing and that I needed to give him time.

He responded that he wished I would have told him this before, he wished we would have talked. He continued to believe I didn't need him, and he felt so alone, which made it easy for him to go back to where he felt needed, to where he was welcomed with open arms.

Then he asked me if it was too late for us, him and me.

Deep breath.

I told him it's never too late, but that I needed to move on. I wasn't going to move back to the city, and I was ready to make a life for the kids and me close to my family. And I told him the same thing I had been telling him for two months: that every day he wakes up with a choice. He could choose the easy path, the path with her where he didn't have to deal with any of his sh*t, or he could choose the harder path, the one that involved facing his emotions, that would ultimately lead to his happiness. And I said that either choice he made was probably not going to be pretty for the next little while.

If he chose to continue on the path he was on, there would likely be more moments of war in our future because we hadn't figured out how to navigate this yet . . . but I believed we would.

And if he chose the path of coming with his family, which I believed was the choice of happiness for him, then it wasn't going to be easy either. We both knew he had a lot of work to do before he could be happy with us.

He responded by saying he didn't want to run anymore. He wanted to face it all. And he asked if he could hop on a train and come to us, leaving everything else behind.

I said no, unfortunately, it wasn't that easy anymore.

But I told him I would be heading back to the city the next day, and he knew where to find me if he wanted to discuss this seriously.

The next night, just as I arrived in the city, I received a text from him asking if I was back home. I said yes, but I would only be there for four days. I was packing everything up, the movers were coming Monday, and then we were gone. He said he would be over first thing the next morning.

He arrived at 6 a.m., and for the next three hours, he just held Sloan in his arms. Kane stayed asleep, and he and I didn't talk. He just held his daughter. It felt different when he held Sloan in that moment, almost as if it was the first time they had met each other.

It didn't matter that we didn't talk; I didn't feel anxious about it. I could feel his heart opening. I could feel the peace, and that told me more than words could convey.

After three hours, he had to go to work, so he handed Sloan over to me and asked if he could come back the next morning. It was clear that being there with us gave him a sense of calm and a sense of peace.

He came back the next day, again picked Sloan up and held her for three hours, just staring into her face. This is when he told me he feels like she is a miracle, an angel who's here to help us heal. I had only heard Craig talk like this once before, on that drive home from my gramma's funeral. The first time he told me he wanted to choose us.

From there, the conversation opened up. We talked about all the things we should have been talking about those past few months. We talked about how we got to the point we were at, how we didn't deal with the babies we lost, how we shut each other out, how we stopped being Jak and Craig and started just being Kane's mom and dad.

He told me he wanted to come with us, wherever we were heading. He said, "I can't live away from you guys." He was willing to give up his life in the city, his job, his relationship, all of it. He wanted to be with us and to be close to my family who had always been so supportive of him and us. And again, he said he wanted to stop running.

Our house in the city was closing in two weeks, and he asked if he could come then. He asked for two weeks to sort things out with his business partner, two weeks to end his relationship, two weeks and then he was prepared to leave the city for good.

The human part of me wanted to say yes.

But my soul said something different, and I had learned not to deny my soul. I was only willing to speak truth and the truth was my soul said no.

It said no to the timeline. I told him I was packing up the house over the weekend. The movers were coming Monday morning to load all of our belongings in a moving truck so we could make it back to my family in time for Thanksgiving dinner.

I told him I had no expectation for him to follow through on what he had just asked for, but if come Monday morning it was what he truly wanted, he could come with us. I told him I didn't care what he did between now and then. He could decide over the weekend, not over two weeks.

He said he'd already decided.

I just said, "We will see."

"We won't see. I promise I'm coming Monday."

He asked if he could stay with us for the next three days. I said no to that too. I wasn't available for the dabbling in and out. I didn't want to place expectations between us. I was at the point where I had fully surrendered to God's plan.

He asked me where I wanted him to stay, and I said, "Stay where you have been staying, stay with her. Give her, and you, closure; don't just run away."

So, that's what he did. He'd already planned to be with our kids during the day on both Saturday and Sunday, but what he did those nights felt like it didn't matter.

I had no attachment to him showing up three days from then, and him staying with her oddly felt like the best place for him to be.

chapter 66 | staying with her

People have asked me to explain, and I've tried. But how do you explain something that doesn't make sense? How do you explain something you just know inside of you?

And I get it. If I were in their shoes, I'd want to understand, how was I okay with it? How was I okay with him going back there after he said he was coming with us? How was I okay with him sleeping with her?

Because I had chosen to live in my truth. And I had decided that his choices would only affect me if I allowed them to.

So, I asked myself questions like: What's in it for me? What am I being called to remember? What am I being called to heal?

And who am I willing to lean into . . . God, or my human ego?

I continued to choose God.
I continued to choose my truth above all else.

And here's the thing about your truth: it may not make sense to others. And that's okay. It's not meant to.

There may be moments when your truth doesn't even make sense to you. Not at the mind level.

But it always makes sense at the level of the soul, which we often only see in hindsight.

chapter 67 | the way of the warrior

We've been raised in societies where surrender is seen as powerlessness, where vulnerability is seen as weak. Un-Godly.

We've been taught to be strong, to fight, to be the warriors. That this is Godly, this is just.

What if we're ready to drop the warrior energy. To put down the fight. To release. To choose peace. To hold the frequency of love.

MY MARRIAGE HAD
THE OPPORTUNITY
TO SURVIVE WHEN I
STOPPED NEEDING
MY MARRIAGE
TO SURVIVE.

chapter 68 | the three days

The first day was what it was; he did his thing, I did mine. I was out with a girlfriend that night, and all I asked was that he didn't show up at the same restaurant as us; that's how close our circles felt.

The second day was what it was, until it wasn't. Craig spent the day with the kids while I was at an event, then he dropped them off in the early evening. He was in a rush when he dropped them off but said he'd be back in an hour.

Something had happened, but I wasn't sure what. I didn't feel safe. My insides were turning. This was not what we had agreed to. I didn't want to hold out hope anymore.

One hour turned into two, turned into three, and then I decided to head to bed. I locked the door to our house, but when I got halfway up the stairs, I felt a soul nudge and turned around to unlock it. This was the second time I'd had this experience.

An hour later, he was there and lay down beside me. He didn't say anything, just held my hand under the sheets. And I knew he had done what he said he was going to do. His other relationship was over.

He woke up the next morning, the third day, to forty-two texts and thirty-seven missed calls. The texts mostly said an iteration of the same thing: She was spiraling without him. She needed him. She begged him to reconsider. She loved him. She told him he would never be happy with me, and that I would never love him like she does. And it ended with she hated him.

I asked him what he wanted to do and he said he was going to shut his phone off and go to Thanksgiving with his family and the kids like he had planned. He asked me if I wanted to go with them. I asked him if he needed me to. If he needed the support, I would go, but if not, I would stay and pack up before the movers came the next day. Taking a day for myself was the most nurturing thing I could do.

He left, I stayed. And when he brought me take-out dinner later that night, I couldn't help but think he'd finally arrived with that Sunday night takeout, only thirty-three weeks late.

When the movers came the next morning, I still didn't trust he was solid in his decision. He said he was, but I also saw the text she'd sent that morning asking for one more chance to talk before he left if that's what he was really going to do.

She said she'd be outside her house waiting on the steps. If he showed up, it would mean one thing to her, that she would know there was hope for them, and if he didn't, she said he wouldn't hear from her again. We both believed her.

The moving van was packed. Craig got in the driver's seat. The kids and I were packed inside our truck. We were ready to hit the road. Craig told me he was shutting his phone off, and we made a plan to meet an hour outside the city to get lunch on our way.

And at that moment, a little bit of fear crept into my head. Would he show up? When it came down to getting on the highway, was he actually going to be able to do it? We both knew she was there, just two blocks away, waiting for him.

I knew it wasn't easy for him to walk away from any of it. Her, the city, his work, the only place he had ever known as home.

The kids and I left a couple minutes before him, but I stopped at the gas station at the corner. I needed gas—but I also stationed myself there so I could spy on him. If Craig turned right at the gas station, he was choosing her. If he went straight, we would all be on our way, driving to a place we knew and into the unknown at the same time.

We had both admitted by this point that we didn't know if we could heal from this. We didn't know if leaving the city together meant we were choosing to be together. We just knew we were willing to figure it out. We would heal together and support each other and let the outcome of our marriage sort itself out.

I had butterflies in my stomach as I saw him approach the intersection, and, of course, he hit a red light. Waiting, waiting, waiting . . . until we saw him go straight. Then the kids and I pulled out behind him.

ANYWHERE
THERE IS NEED,
THERE IS
ALSO A LIE.

chapter 69 | the need to know

In the beginning, I was desperate to hang on to my marriage because I had bought into the illusion of need.

I thought we needed to stay married in order to thrive.
I thought I needed it.
My husband needed it.
My kids needed it.

The need for my marriage to survive created a distortion in my desire for my marriage to survive. It tainted the frequency. It led me down a path of control, manipulation, and desperation.

It led me to put my human agenda ahead of my soul's agenda.

But what would have happened if this need didn't exist?
What would have happened if I didn't need a particular outcome?

I wouldn't have suffered.
I wouldn't have been consumed with fear and worry.
I wouldn't have wanted to tell God to go f*ck himself.

Need is an illusion, and God does not have an agenda for you—you do.
You have a human agenda, and because of this, you believe there are things you need.

Things you need in order to survive.
Things you need in order to be happy.
Things you need in order to experience abundance.
Things you need in order to be successful.
Things you need in order to find love.

Need at the core does not exist.

Need is a man-made concept.

How do I know this? That need doesn't exist, that need is an illusion?

Because God has no needs, therefore we cannot have any needs. This is true at a human level and at a soul level.

There is nothing you need to experience here, nothing that you're even meant to experience here other than the truth that you are meant to experience that in which you truly are. You are meant to experience yourself as the creator, as the one. You are meant to be the fullest expression of who you know yourself to be at a soul level.

Often, we buy into the illusion that things are meant to happen or not to happen because it helps us make sense of things.

God meant it to happen = God has preferences = God has needs = God has wants that are separate from your wants.

This is not true.

Our tendency to need to know how everything is going to work out is an attempt to control God. An attempt to find certainty. An attempt to hedge our bets. An insurance policy, so to speak.

If I can figure God out . . .
If I can figure love out . . .
If I can figure money out . . .

. . . then I will know the rules.
. . . then I will understand the game.
. . . then I can win.
. . . then I will be happy.

But it's in our need to figure it out. We complicate most things.

We buy into the illusion of need in order to be happy. We create man-made rules, timelines, and formulas that construct limitations in our energy field. This is why you don't have the things you want. It's not because you can't have them, it's because you believe you can't. You haven't figured it out, and therefore you believe you are not worthy or deserving.

Oh, the lies you tell yourself.

Life is much simpler than that when you know, when you understand, when you embrace yourself as the creator.

You are the creator.
Everything you desire is available to you.

It already exists.
You are here to experience heaven on earth.

Polarity is a requirement. It leads to the power of choice. It allows you to enact your own free will, allowing you to experience yourself as the creator, as the one, part of God. Which is ultimately exactly what you came here to do. It's why you chose to come into human form, to experience that who you truly are.

As a soul, it's not possible to experience who you truly are. As a soul, you know you are a divine being.

You know truth.
You know love.
You know joy.
You know bliss.
You know abundance.

In the realm of the soul, that is all that exists. Only light exists, which makes it impossible to experience lightness or darkness. Light simply exists because it is. In its pure form, pure truth. So, to experience light, not just know light, your soul chooses to come into human form. To experience that which you know amongst the contrast of that which you are not.

The problem is, as you arrive on earth, you tend to forget that you know, and so begins the journey of remembering. Remembering who you truly are. Knowing that within each opposite that presents itself, you have the opportunity to choose to align with the truth of your soul.

When darkness appears, you have the opportunity to choose light. Amidst hate, you can choose love.
You can choose condemnation or non-judgment.
You can choose hopelessness or faith.

Through these words, I'm inviting you into remembrance.

I'm guiding you to meet and connect with the truth within you. To remember your soul's knowing, to remember that which you've forgotten.

But also remember this:

You came here because you wanted to do more than know what your soul knows. You wanted to experience what your soul knows. To fully do so, embrace all aspects of being human.

Embrace the failures, the f*ck ups, the disappointments, the hurt, the heartbreak, the losses. For each experience is truly a gift, even when you can't see it. Each experience is an opportunity for you to go deeper in your remembrance. Each experience is an opportunity for you to choose to be that who you truly are.

Each experience always opens a doorway to "this or something better."

Your actions, reactions, and belief codes determine what comes next. Do you walk through the doorway that God has so graciously opened? Or do you slam the door in God's face?

PART FOUR

the transcendence

chapter 70 | because of that

I grew up going to church every Sunday.

Because of that, I learned about a God who punishes, judges, and condemns.

Because of that, I left the church when I was twelve.

Because of that, I no longer felt connected to the word God.

Because of that, I started to explore what spirituality meant to me.

Because of that, I started to believe in something, but I wasn't sure what.

Because of that, I started to use the word "universe" and talk to angels . . . not God, but angels.

Because of that, I connected to an energy outside of me.

Because of that, I toe-dipped in and out of spirituality for years . . . believing, but unsure, witnessing miracles, but not understanding.

Because of that, I sometimes listened and sometimes didn't . . . we're talking about listening to the voice inside of me.

Because of that, I ignored God when she came knocking.

Because of that, I woke up when he knocked so loudly I couldn't ignore him.

Because of that, I went on a deep inward journey.

Because of that, I found God within me.

Because of that, I cultivated a level of trust and a level of faith that is unwavering.

Because of that, I became unwilling to deny my soul.

Because of that, I became devoted to speaking my truth.

Because of that, I became the fullest expressed version of myself.

Because of that, I started to deliver my medicine to thousands of humans.

Because of that, I am now dedicated to reaching millions.

Because of that, I'm writing this book.

Because of that, I am allowing God to speak through me.

Because of that, I am who I came here to be.

chapter 71 | the letter to HER

It had been a week since we left the city. He hadn't heard from her and he didn't expect to. When he didn't turn right that day, when he chose to come with us, she said she hated him, that he ruined her life, and she was going to forget he ever existed.

He assumed she blocked him, and he said he had no intention of contacting her again anyway. But when his phone pinged and I saw the color drain from his face, I knew she'd made contact. He read the message and then handed the phone to me.

It was a long email that started off in anger, somewhere in the middle came vulnerability, and it ended with her telling him that when he was there, she woke up every morning knowing he wasn't there to stay, that they weren't going to last forever, despite what they both promised each other. She knew all along she was just a toy.

This situation wasn't easy on any of us. I knew he wanted to be where he was, with us, but he was also having a hard time dealing with the aftermath of the choices he'd made the last seven months. She wasn't just a toy. I knew what she meant to him; he never wanted to hurt her. He put a lot of blame on himself, not knowing how to deal with the feeling that he "put us all through so much for nothing," and that he'd hurt two people he loved in the process.

As I read the email for myself, my mind told me it was a manipulation of his emotions. After seven months of doing everything she could to separate him from his family, asking him not to attend his daughter's birth, she told him that if he would have come back that day, if he had given her a chance that morning before we drove off in the moving truck, she was going to tell him she was willing to make sure his kids, our kids, were included in their life. She said she was willing to accept that his kids were his priority, and she wasn't going to make him choose anymore.

While the human part of me told me that the email was meant to manipulate him and to invoke guilt in him, my soul told me something different. My soul, my heart, my truth felt compassion for her. I hurt for her. I wanted to reach out to her. I thought about doing so many times. I wrote her an email, but then didn't send it. I told myself I was the last person she wanted to hear from. Truth be told, I wasn't brave enough. I didn't because I was afraid I wouldn't be received the way I intended, and I was afraid of being rejected. I knew during some moments, at least, she had chosen to see me as the villain.

So, I wrote the letter and then instead of sending it to her, I posted it online. Our circles were small enough that I assumed it would get to her, and if not, I hoped that she somehow energetically felt the essence of my message.

BLOG POST

You weren't a toy; you were loved. You were treated the way you deserve to be treated—with kindness, generosity, and love. Craig is my husband and I know how much he loved you, how much he loves you. Don't let the outcome of this situation close your heart off to love. You once said he treated you like a queen . . . remember that feeling. That's how you deserve to be treated. I know there is a lesson for each of us in all that we have experienced these past few months. I pray that your lesson is to remember you are worthy of love.

chapter 72 | what if . . .

What if at the end of your life your movie is played back to you.

Every choice, every action, every word, every thought.
In pure form, in pure truth.

If you were able to see where you betrayed yourself, where you held back, where you played to not lose, where fear stopped you, where the idea of judgment stopped you, where the illusion of guilt and shame stopped you . . .

And what if you not only see your life through the lens of your own eyes but also through others as well. The lens of how what you said/did/chose, how it affected your child, your partner, your sibling, your friend, your enemy, that stranger.

What if you lived your life knowing at the end you'd get to watch it all again?

What experiences would you choose now?
What would you create?
How would you move?

And are you brave enough to do it?
To choose it?

chapter 73 | praying for HER

A month or so later, when we heard she had a near-death experience during a car accident, I prayed for her. Yes, it felt weird, of course it did; at a very human level, it felt so weird. I didn't know why I felt called to do so. I was pretty sure if I told anyone, they would think I was nuts. I could hear them in my mind saying, "After all she did to you and your family."

But the thing is, that was all in my mind.
And yes, maybe they would have said it, if I told them.

But it wasn't about them. I'm not even entirely sure it was about her. It felt like it was about me and her, both of us, and a previous version of me.

So, while it was weird on the human level, at a soul level, it felt natural. It felt, of course, in a completely opposite way.

I prayed for her because I wanted her to stay on this earth for long enough to experience love in the way I know we're all here to experience it. A love that first comes from within us and then extends out.

In praying for her, I was also praying for me, and ultimately, us. All of us: you plus me, plus the person sitting beside you at this very moment.

Praying that each and every one of us lives to know the love that we are here to experience, the love that we are here to give, the love that we are here to be, the love that we're here to receive *freely*. As children of God, as the loving essence we are made of.

As the holy ones.
As the chosen ones.

Each and every one of us who self-selected. Who chose this soul mission of coming to earth at this moment in time. To be the fullest expression of who we truly are. To be love. To bring light. To stand in conviction of who we are.

In unity.
As one.

I am because I am.
You are because you are.

I am because you are.
You are because I am.

We meet where truth plus truth intersects. Your truth unlocks my truth; my truth unlocks your truth. And not because your truth and my truth are the same. No, we both know and can allow multiple truths to coexist.

Through me speaking my truth, you remember, you find your truth.
Through you speaking your truth, I remember, I find my truth.

It's a divine dance. Truth weaving truth. Remembrance leading to remembrance.

Therefore, we both, we all, each and every one of us, must be willing to know our truth, stand in our truth, live our truth, speak our truth, be our truth. And to share it with others.

chapter 74 | the excavation

The part where Craig and I reconciled did not come easy. Not for either of us, but certainly not for him. At this point, there were no Band-Aid solutions on the table. I truly wasn't sure what came next for him and me together. But I knew I would be there to support him in his healing journey.

When we left the city, we began to see a human performance coach who also specialized in marriage counseling. We saw him together, and Craig saw him individually as well.

The first question he asked us when we arrived was whether we loved each other. We both said yes.

The second question he asked was if we both wanted to remain married. We both said yes.

Those would be the only two easy questions.
He told us the road that lay ahead for us would likely not be easy.

He asked me if I was sure.
I said yes.

And the deep excavation began.

A lot of pain was brought forth during those sessions. A lot of tears. A lot of facing some deep harsh realities. It's not how I ever would have imagined spending the first few months of my daughter's life.

Exactly four months into our healing journey, four months after Sloan was born, there was another experience for us to heal through together. I had my third miscarriage in the span of three years.

This time, we didn't bury our feelings. We talked.

We talked about our fears and dreams.
We talked about our sadness and our joy.
We talked about our pain and our pleasure.

And I realized something powerful about pain.

Pain isn't meant to be avoided. It's part of the human experience. Pain isn't here or brought forth to cause more pain. The pain is brought forth to be transcended.

Pain transcended to understanding.
Pain transcended to compassion.
Pain transcended to forgiveness.
Pain transcended to love.
Pain transcended to truth.

We fear the pain being brought forth. But what's more to fear is the pain remaining hidden. Pain brought to the light gets transmuted.

PAIN
BROUGHT
FORTH
GETS
HEALED.

chapter 75 | the tattoo

What about the tattoo? The one with her initials on his ring finger.

He didn't just cover it up or put a mask over it. He went through the long process and pain of having it removed. It was a long process because the ink had to be brought to the surface layer by layer, then treated, then it needed time to heal. Then it needed to be repeated all over again.

It took almost two years of this cycle. The pain—healing—pain—healing cycle.

This felt reflective of our healing journey together. There was no just covering it up, there were no masks, there was no bypassing.

We faced it, bringing all aspects of the human experience and soul journey forward. We sat in sacred witness of it all, and eventually, the removal was complete.

That day in the park when I said the first time he left it was for me, the second time it was for you, I also wrote these words underneath:

"SHE CONQUERED HER DEMONS AND WORE HER SCARS LIKE WINGS."

–ATTICUS

chapter 76 | it is because it is

For me, it's quite simple.

I believe what I believe . . .
I know what I know . . .
And it is because it is . . .

I'm not willing to live any other way.

I trust because I choose to trust.

I'm not willing to dabble in the energy of maybe they're right and I'm wrong.

My truth is my truth.
Just like your truth is your truth.

I don't second-guess it.
I don't question myself.
I don't doubt what I know.
I don't overcomplicate it by needing to explain it.

It's true because I believe it to be so.

It's so clear to me.
It's so obvious to me.

It's clear and obvious that who I am, what I know, and what I choose gets to be the thing that creates tidal waves of beauty in my life.

It's clear to me that who you are gets to do the same.

You get to bring your desires into manifestation.
You get to go from zero to one hundred—to one million in an instant.
You get to skip steps.

It's not necessary for you to operate in ways that make sense.
Logical mindset and logical timelines get to be dismantled.

You get to be bold.
You get to do it your way.

In full ownership of who you are.

You lead.
You decide the frequency you play in.
You invite God to meet you on the playground.

YOU.
It's always been you.
It will always be you.

chapter 77 | remembrance

My forgiveness wasn't about not remembering; it was about remembering. Remembering that he is human and divine. Remembering that she is human and divine. Remembering that I am human and divine.

Remembering that he has his soul agenda, she has her soul agenda, and I have mine.

Remembering that each and every one of us is here navigating this soul journey and human experience in the way we know best, with the tools we've been given, with the upbringing we've had, with the traumas we carry.

And remembering this was never about me, and never about us.

His choice was not about me. I was not "cheated on." I am not a victim. He made a choice. He had an affair. And like everything I've come to realize, it had nothing to do with me and everything to do with me at the same time.

THE POSSIBILITY OF BEING
THE VICTIM IS ALWAYS THERE
FOR YOU TO CHOOSE.
BUT WHEN YOU CHOOSE
TO SEE THROUGH THE ILLUSION
OF VICTIMHOOD,
IT BECOMES THE
LAUNCHING PAD FOR

*THE GODDESS
TO BE BORN.*

chapter 78 | the human mind

The human mind is powerful. It's so powerful it can almost convince you of anything. It can convince you into something aligned for you—it can convince you into something not aligned for you.

And while the human mind is extraordinary and beneficial in many ways, when it comes to divine remembrance, when it comes to soul-knowing, when it comes to expanding into the realm of wild potentiality, it's not.

When it comes to mastering the energetics in the unknown, it's not.

This is where the human mind can create massive limitations in your energy field, limiting what you're available for and ultimately, limiting what you cocreate and receive.

And the thing is, it's so easy to get caught up in the chatter and noise of our human mind. Especially as many of us have been conditioned to do so.

We've been trained . . .

To think things through.
To use our head.
To make the right choice.
To weigh the pros and cons.
To analyze and then analyze some more.
To make it make sense.
To not f*ck it up.

But here's the thing: Your human mind only knows what it currently knows. It only knows based on past experiences, past memories, past stories it has been told.

So, when you want to expand in new realms and new possibilities, your mind is not your ally.

This is why it's essential to train your soul voice to speak louder than your human mind.

Your soul voice is the voice that comes from the depth within. It's that deep intuitive wisdom, the one that nudges you to go left when you thought you'd go right. The one that nudges you to do the thing, even though the pathway is uncertain.

It's often the voice that doesn't make sense and makes perfect sense at the same time.

And it's the voice you're meant to listen to.

Because when you do, when you move with this voice, when you trust in this voice, you access that which lives beyond anything your human mind can comprehend.

The truth is there waiting for you.
It's up to you to be willing to access it.

chapter 79 | my soul-knowing

We spoke at length about the conflict between my soul knowing our story wasn't over and his desperation to speed up the ending of us. And although it was the thing he wanted most at the time, the thing he said on repeat, that he wanted our marriage to be over, there were signs that at a soul level, he felt differently. He ignored it, but I owned it.

I had felt this truth over and over again, and throughout the seven months of our separation, I was willing to express it.

I said earlier that "the most important truth you will ever express is the truth of who you are."

Let's dive deeper in this.

Each and every one of us is a child of God, the voice of God, the creator as God. God lives within us. As such, we each hold sacred wisdom and sacred codes within us. We hold these codes; we are the keepers of the truth—the truth that is not meant to be held on to or meant to be kept hidden but is meant to be expressed.

No one knows more about who you are than you. No one is the authority on you. No one is your guru. No one holds power over you. No one's truth is more true than your truth. You are the one God chooses to express through. You are chosen, as I am chosen, as we are chosen. We choose and, in turn, are the chosen ones.

There is no hierarchy here.
No pedestal.
No better than.
No more deserving.
No more worthy.

At a soul level, you know this. At a human level, you give your power away on the regular to people you think know more, to the ones who have it figured out, the ones who are more successful than you, the ones who you believe talk to God not understanding you can too, to the people you believe are the way.

You are the way.
The only way.
The one.

You also give your power away to a God who lives outside of you when you look to him to "fix it." "Let go and let God" is not the way if it leaves you feeling powerless, or like the victim, or like the one who is not capable.

Let go and let God in its most potent expression is a surrender within, knowing that there are things you can't possibly see through your limited human lens.

Let go and let God represents the willingness to have faith beyond measure, to trust in what you can't yet see. To surrender in service of your highest good and the highest good of others.

Not because you are powerless—no, because you are powerful.

WE HAVE THE POWER
TO AWAKEN THE GOD/
GODDESS, THE SOURCE
OF LOVE, WITHIN US.
AND BEYOND THAT,
WE HAVE THE POWER
TO AWAKEN THE GOD/
GODDESS, THE SOURCE
OF LOVE,
WITHIN OTHERS.

chapter 80 | divine timing

I believe in divine timing, and I don't believe time is real.
Not in the way we know it.
Linear timelines are man-made.

So, with this in mind, what does divine timing even mean?

It means that the time in which anything happens is divine.
So, why force it? Why push? Why over complicate it? Why push it further away with your human doubt and worry?

The tide will be high, when the tide is high.
The tide will be low, when the tide is low.
The tide comes in, and the tide goes out.
This is the frequency of divine timing.

God isn't holding back when the tide's low. God's not saying, I don't want them to experience that right now. It simply is what it is. It is part of divine nature.

So, if divine timing is not God holding back on you; if God doesn't have a timeline, an agenda, a need or requirement for you, then what?

You're free to open up to the truth that the divine moment, the divine timing, might be now. It might be tomorrow, it might be soon, it might be not so soon. And it doesn't matter; you don't need to control it.

You drop into the frequency of allowance.
Trusting in timing more than time itself.
This is what divine timing is.

It's knowing that things are happening behind the scenes that you can't yet see with your human eyes. It's knowing that your belief in its existence—it being the desire—is what draws it closer and leads to you experiencing it in the human realm.

It's knowing that the moment the prayer is voiced is the moment it is answered.

This is where you're called to stand in conviction.
To not waver.

Knowing who you are as a divine creator.
Not because you have the evidence but because you have steadfast faith.

Not being attached to time and seeing divinity's hand in everything, God's hand in everything.

It's knowing it's all happening for you, even when it looks like it's not. Even when it looks like it may never come. Even when the opposite appears.

If you don't buy into the distortion that that which you desire doesn't exist, if you see all of it as part of the journey, and all of it as serving your soul's agenda . . .

If you trust things are always in motion, moving you toward the experiencing of that which you desire . . .

It will happen when it happens. And what happens in between will be in service of your soul's agenda as well.

chapter 81 | eight years later

The story doesn't end here. In the last eight years, there have been periods of healing, growth, normalcy, growing businesses, raising humans, and committing together and on our own to our spiritual growth and evolution.

We've packed up our kids for an extended road trip and ended up accidentally moving across the country. We've unschooled our kids and also enrolled them in nature school, Spirit school, and art school. We currently spend half the year on the beach in the jungle of Costa Rica and the other half in the mountains on the west coast of Canada.

Over the past eight years, I've devoted myself to teaching, guiding, and mentoring women on their own inward journey. Connecting them to the sacred wisdom within them. The God within. The Divine within. The medicine within.

I've studied *Conversations with God* by Neale Donald Walsch. I've studied scripture in the gospels of Mary Magdalene. But mostly, I've "learned" by sitting in communion with myself, by trusting the truth that comes from within me, by understanding that my soul knows things that my human cannot yet comprehend, by surrendering the need to know and the desire to control. By seeing the illusions that we, as humans, tend to get so caught up in, and by transcending that which creates lack and limitation in my world.

I consciously choose to return to love again and again and again.
I invite God to meet me where I desire to be met.
I speak freely, lead freely, and teach freely.

In devotion to me. In devotion to you.

When "the work" feels hard between my husband and me, we remind each other that either we face it, heal it, and recode it, or we leave it to our children. We know it's up to us to disrupt the patterns and to practice what we preach.

Recently, I was asked what I'm most proud of in my life and I said me. I'm the most proud of me. I'm also incredibly proud of us.

For our willingness to choose love when it was hard. For recoding and continuing to recode the millions of patterns and cycles we find ourselves in. For rewriting the story, not just for us but for the generations to come after us. For all of the hard conversations. For all of the choices. For the way we now choose to live . . . fully alive, with deep devotion to who we both are as individuals and to the unit we've created together.

It's taken a lot to get here. Our love has been unpredictable. The life we live is unpredictable.

And it's exactly why it works for us. Because we choose it again and again and again.

When it's easy.
When it's hard.

When it makes sense.
And when it doesn't.

I'm far from perfect, but I know I am doing my very best. I know with every part of my being that the things I experience, the thoughts I have, the uploads, the downloads, the channeled wisdom, the truth I feel inside me is not just meant for me, it's meant for you too.

Our wisdom is meant to be shared, mine and yours.
Our medicine is meant to be shared.

Sharing is what connects us.

This is not to say that we are ever not connected. But storytelling and sharing in this way reminds us that we are always connected. It reminds us that we are not so different, you, me, him, and her.

We all have our part to play. We all have a unique soul journey. But we are all, at the core, one.

You are me.
And I am you.

We are God.
God is us.

All exists because you exist.
All exists because I exist.

This is a truth your soul already knows.

You came here of your choosing.
You will leave here of your choosing.

Truth cannot be taken from you.
Life cannot be taken from you.
Love cannot be taken from you.

You change form, but your soul is everlasting.

You have not been forsaken.
You have not been forgotten.

It's not even possible.

You are a child of God.
A child of the universe.
A child of the heavens.
An angel in human form.

chapter 82 | god's rules

Throughout this Spiritual Smackdown, I said God no-optioned me, but what truly happened was I no-optioned me.

God doesn't no-option us.
God doesn't test us.

We do that to ourselves. My soul called it forth.
Not this experience, in this way, but I asked God to awaken me.

I asked for the divine remembrance to be sparked within me.

I just didn't see it until I looked back in hindsight, seeing all the soul nudges being pieced together.

God doesn't have an agenda for us. There is nothing that we are meant to experience here. There is nothing we are supposed to learn.

Throughout this Spiritual Smackdown, and for a few years following, I believed that this experience was meant to happen in my life. I believed that Craig and Hannah were always destined to meet and destined to have an affair. It served me during this experience to believe that it allowed me to not make it about me.

I no longer think that.

Maybe they were always destined to meet, but I don't think their relationship was always destined. We all have free will here. Nothing is already set in stone. If Craig and I were in a different spot in our journey together, if we had learned to communicate in healthier ways, if we had grieved the loss of our babies together, then the pathway to their relationship may not have been open. All three of us had previously made choices in our life that led to that pathway being open at that moment in time.

God didn't make it happen, but he allowed it to happen. And it served each of us deeply, in many ways.

To believe God tests us means we believe in a God that doesn't truly exist. It means we continue to believe the rules. Let's revisit them now and reveal the truth. The truth that you already know.

Rule #1: There must be someone between you and God, a master who can translate, so to speak.

Truth: You are a direct channel to God. God lives within you, not outside of you. You are never not connected. You and God are one.

Rule #2: You must obey God.

Truth: God doesn't command you. You command God. You serve God when you allow God to serve you.

Rule #3: Sacrifice is essential.

Truth: Love is essential, nothing else.

Rule #4: God has specific wants for you, and they are very different from your wants.

Truth: God wants what you want. If the desire exists within you, it's available to you. You have free will. You are always free to choose.

Rule #5: God knows and you don't.

Truth: Your soul knows, your soul remembers, it's your human that's forgotten. Get still enough to listen and you will remember. I know because I know, because I know, will be sparked within you.

Rule #6: The devil exists. Be afraid.

Truth: Heaven is real, Hell isn't. Sin doesn't exist. Death doesn't exist. There is nothing to be afraid of. Fear is an illusion.

Rule #7: God has a plan for you. You better be a good girl and follow it.

Truth: God has no agenda for you, outside of you experiencing yourself as the truth of who you are: the creator; heaven in human form.

Rule #8: There are certain things you must do and not do in order to get to heaven.

Truth: There is no good and bad, right or wrong. There is no condemnation. God doesn't sit at the gates of heaven judging you, he embraces you home with open arms.

THE MEANING
OF EACH EVENT
IN OUR LIFE
IS THE MEANING
WE GIVE IT.

This is not connected to a rule, but it is truth in its purest form.

chapter 83 | words from my husband

Midway through writing this book, I asked myself the question: Do you really want to share this story? Do you really want to publish this knowing that it is very likely that one day our children will read it?

And then I remembered something my husband said to me eight years ago when I first told him I wanted to write this book: "I'm okay with it. It's part of our story; tell it if you want to."

"How would you feel about our kids one day reading it?"

"I'm fine with it. I want them to know that there will be times they f*ck up, there will be times they make mistakes, and they will still be loved."

And with that I continued to write, because this story is bigger than him, bigger than me, bigger than us.

I GIVE
ZERO F*CKS
AND
A MILLION F*CKS
ALL AT
THE SAME TIME.
*IT FUELS
MY MOVEMENT.*

chapter 84 | truth frequency

Now more than ever we're being called to step into our authentic truth.

In unapologetic ownership of who we are.
In unwavering conviction.
In full self-expression.

Illusions are being dismantled, as we are becoming truly available to see that which we haven't seen before.

Truth frequency cannot be disrupted. But untruth can.

Untruths are being broken down. Distortions are being revealed.

Self-imposed limitations are being shattered.

More and more we are waking up in remembrance to the divine essence that flows within EACH and EVERY ONE OF US.

Stepping forward to take radical responsibility for what we are creating at conscious and subconscious levels.

Individually and Collectively.

I CHOOSE
LOVE.

final thought | unconditional happiness

Happiness is a choice. I am not happy because I am strong. I am not happy because I put blinders on. I am not happy because Instagram makes the world think my life is perfect. I am happy because I choose to be happy.

You also have the freedom to choose.

Choose to live in the moment.
Choose to extract the lessons from your journey.
Choose to not see these as lessons at all but divine remembrance.

Choose to see life as a gift.
Choose to trust the universe has your back.
Choose to have faith that God is conspiring in your favor.

afterword

When I began writing this book, I was encouraged by a spiritual mentor who I have a deep, profound respect for. Reading his books have been the catalyst to much of my growth. Every time I read his words, and every time we have conversations, I drop deeper into the divine remembrance of who I am.

When he told me he believed that this book was going to be a powerful book that would transform many people's lives, I felt the depth of truth in his words. I heard God's voice speaking through him.

And this is what sparked my desire to finally put pen to paper, just like God had called me to do many years before. It was time. He knew it. I knew it. God knew it.

And I became further motivated when in front of a room full of people, this mentor made a promise to me. He used the word "promise"; to me it felt like a pact between him, me, and God. A promise/pact that once I was finished writing this manuscript, he would not only write the foreword for the book, but he would also personally deliver it to his literary agent of many, many years.

He said he knew they would "flip out over it."

God was winking at me in this moment . . . a foreword by a well-known author and spiritual mentor—an effortless handoff to a trusted literary agent—backed with the belief that they would easily find a publisher to bring my story to the world. It felt divinely orchestrated.

But neither of those things happened. The foreword didn't happen. The handoff to the literary agent didn't happen.

And there is a story behind the why of this that I feel compelled to share with you.

Once the book was written, I sent my mentor my manuscript. A manuscript I felt incredibly proud of. For years I told myself this book needed to be written by someone else, because for years I told myself I wasn't a writer. And here I was, hitting send on the first draft of my first-ever manuscript. It wasn't edited. I wanted my raw, vulnerable voice of truth to be heard as it was, as I experienced it.

His initial response was that the book is "emotionally captivating, an arresting read, and filled with great wisdom." But a few short weeks later, he did a 180 and shared that he felt this book was a "great shaming" of my husband and that it would cause irrevocable harm to my children and their relationship with their father. Ultimately, he said he wanted to endorse this book because of the wisdom in it, but he also wanted me to remove the story aspect of the book. "To let the depth of wisdom stand on its own."

He said the story wasn't needed. He wanted me to erase the experience of infidelity completely. I shed tears as I listened to his words because I knew what I once thought would be, wouldn't be. I understood what he was saying, but I completely disagreed. I knew I wasn't willing to compromise my truth in this.

Because the erasure of the story felt like a complete erasure of the book.

The wisdom exists because the story exists.
Because I lived it.

As a mentor, I lead and teach through my lived wisdom; I don't hide parts of me. Is infidelity an experience that I wish didn't exist in my life or my marriage? Absolutely. And at the same time, I wouldn't change it.

I remembered who I am through this experience.

I remembered who he is, she is, you are, we are through this experience.

I would not be the woman I am today without having this story in my life.

And yes, I have thought many, many times about the potential harm this could cause my children, but each time I do, I go back to my husband's words: "I want them to know that there will be times they f*ck up, there will be times they make mistakes, and they will still be loved."

And ultimately, the truth is, this is something I never thought we'd hide from our kids anyway. Sure, we could, they would never remember. But I understand the codes that get passed down through our lineage. They would then hold the code of shame, the code that some things are meant to be kept hidden, and the code that love is conditional.

I am not willing to do that to them.

I want them to know that one experience in our life doesn't define us. God is always there. There is always an invitation to return to love. And they get to choose.

Again and again and again, they get to choose to remember the truth of their soul's nature.

I was called to many things within this experience. I was called . . .

To choose my soul-knowing above all else.
To trust that my way is the way.

To own who I am.
To reclaim my voice.

To decide that I am the authority in my life.

I decided that I was not willing to compromise my truth, my voice, or the power of my lived wisdom. I was not willing to dull the story down, to dilute the frequency. I was not willing to allow my voice to be silenced. I was not willing to allow shame or judgment to create interference.

I decided I was willing to Let Go and Let God. Trusting in the unfolding I couldn't yet see.

Because being the fullest expression of who I am, being the truth of who I am, is exactly what my soul came here to do.

This is our holy work.
Yours and mine.

It is our holy work to be the truth of who we are. To use our God-given voices and God-given medicine to heal the world.

And I don't say that lightly . . .

Every time you open your mouth. Every time you're willing to speak it.
Your voice—your truth—heals the world.

You are here to be the fullest expression of who you are, and everything you experience in this lifetime is a source for your liberation.

Let truth burn as your eternal flame.
Always.

JACLYN SHAW

In a world of spiritual teachers, Jaclyn Shaw stands apart as a powerful voice for women who are ready to reclaim who they are as divine beings. When Jaclyn speaks, women listen. Her conviction commands attention. Her wisdom resonates at a soul level. Her trust in self and trust in God is undeniably felt.

Through her words, her presence, her embodied teachings and lived wisdom, women tap into the divine remembrance of who they are. They feel the resonance of truth deep in their souls and it becomes the catalyst for their own personal transformation.

In Jaclyn's world, it's not about becoming but returning—returning to your divine nature and the sacred wisdom that lives within you. Truth burns as her eternal flame and faith resonates as her unwavering frequency.

Through profound—yet simple—soul transmissions, she extends an irresistible invitation to women every-where: recognize that you, indeed, are the source of wisdom you've been seeking.

This memoir is my sacred offering to the world. It's a book I hope you come back to again and again and again. I hope you've underlined the parts that hit you in your soul; I hope you've folded the corners so that you remember to come back.

I deeply believe that I lived this experience so that I could carry this wisdom. So that I could crack the codes first for me, and, in turn, for you. To create freedom from limitation and liberation from the lies that we tell ourselves about who we are and why we are here.

You are a child of GOD.
You are heaven in human form.

And you didn't come here to navigate this journey alone. We came to walk it together—to remember, to rise, and to reclaim. This book is only the beginning.

What awaits you next is not just more information, but a living transmission—mentorship, teachings, and sacred containers designed to activate the fullness of who you are.

If these words stirred something deep within you … if you felt the remembrance of your own divinity rising as you read . . . consider this your invitation.

Your next step begins now. Step through the doorway. Continue the journey.

Scan the QR code to access Jaclyn's world of mentorship, transmissions, and community—and experience the deeper work that your soul is calling for.

This is a free activation that will shift your entire frequency.

You will walk away deeper into your power. Into your knowing and into your truth.

Scan it now as my gift to you.

⊙ @jaclyn_shaw_

🎙 Podcast: The Jaclyn Shaw Show

⊕ www.jaclynshaw.ca

IT'S NOT ABOUT GENTLE SPIRITUALITY—IT'S ABOUT RADICAL DIVINE REMEMBRANCE AND THE CALL TO CONNECT TO GOD/THE GODDESS FREQUENCY.

acknowledgments

Thank you first to you, the reader. Sharing the truth about my life and the lived wisdom I've extracted from it is a deep soul calling of mine. Thank you for being here to receive it.

Thank you to Melanie Ann Layer, who has not only been an incredible mentor and confidante in my life but also a champion of my voice and my work. One of my favorite chapters in this book, Chapter 70 | Because of That, comes directly from her teachings. She originated the "because of that" framework, and when she shared her own story using this approach, it inspired me to apply it to my own life and include it in this book.

Thank you to Sabrina Greer and the entire team at fEMPOWER Publications for going above and beyond to make sure every detail of this book was presented in the exact way I envisioned it.

Thank you to all the advance readers who poured so much love into me in the weeks leading up to the release of this memoir.

Thank you to the entire Alpha Femme Team, with special mentions to Melanie, Fred, Shannon, and Amy for making the celebration of this book the most iconic night of my life.

Thank you to my soul sisters Alison, Amy, Brett, Catie, Catherine, Laura, Lindsey, Robyn, and Sarah who held and guided me during this period of my life. First when I birthed Sloan into this world and again as I birthed this book into the world.

And a deeply heartfelt thank you to each and every one of my family members for your support and the extraordinary blessing that you are in my life.

xx Jaclyn